WISDOM FROM THE FRIENDS OF ALLAH

# Jafar as-Sadiq

Rahmatullahi Alayh

Osman Nuri Topbaş

ERKAM PUBLICATIONS

*This Edition is distributed by Ummah Reads, a FKB Publishing Solutions Company*

# *Jafar as-Sadiq*

(Rahmatullahi Alayh)

Osman Nuri Topbaş

**Original Title:** Câfer-i Sâdık (rahmetullâhi aleyh)
**Author :** Osman Nuri Topbaş
**Translator :** El Mahdi Rezoug
**Redactor :** Süleyman Derin
Ömer Wills
**Graphics :** Rasim Şakiroğlu

**Address :** Ikitelli Organize Sanayi Bölgesi Mah.
Atatürk Bulvarı, Haseyad 1. Kısım
No: 60/3-C Başakşehir, Istanbul, Turkey
**Tel :** (90-212) 671-0700 pbx
**Fax :** (90-212) 671-0748
**E-mail :** info@islamicpublishing.org
**Web site :** www.islamicpublishing.org
**Language :** English

ERKAM PUBLICATIONS

Istanbul 1443 / 2022

Content Page can be accessed at the End of the Book

# PREFACE

All praises are due to Allah, the Exalted who has created us, the weak servants of Him by His grace and favor. He has chosen us among the creation to be human beings and from all humanity to be from the Community of the Prophet Muhammad (pbuh), honoring us with the blessings of Islam, Iman (belief) and the Qur'an.

May endless peace and blessings be upon our Beloved Prophet Muhammad who is the guide in this world and our intercessor on the Day of Judgment. May endless peace and blessings be upon his blessed household and Companions.

**Dear honorable brothers and sisters!**

All of us are passing through divine trials in various ways in this temporal world. It is our state and behaviors during the events that we encounter today that determine our station in the divine court tomorrow.

In other words, whether our real life in the hereafter will be an eternal bliss for us or an eternal disaster -May Allah protect us from that- is determined by our conduct in this life.

The Almighty Lord, whose mercy proceeds His wrath, has invited us to a never ending paradise and bliss by sending us the guidance we need from His Prophets, Divine Books and with the aid of those scholars and friends of Allah, who followed the guidance and exemplified it, and who are the inheritors of Prophets.

The friends of Allah are representatives of the Prophetic guidance and perfect character, spread over time. Their warnings and advice are abundant manifestations springing from the Prophet's (pbuh) teaching. The source of spiritual benefit in their gatherings is none other than the blessed Prophet himself (pbuh).

Throughout history, societies have always found peace due to the friends of Allah who are the people of heart. For their Sufi gathering places have served as rehabilitation centers for the exhausted, sad, lonely and wounded hearts. Suspicion and doubt in the hearts of people were replaced by certainty and happiness thanks to the breaths of mercy blowing from those gatherings. Egotistic desires were replaced by spiritual yearning and aspiration with their blessed guidance. The thorns of enmity and animosity were removed from the hearts and the bonds of love and brotherhood blossomed. Many families and friendships that were about to fall apart were revived by them and bridges of compassion and  between the hearts.

In short, societies lived in peace as long as they were benefiting from the guidance of scholars and wise people of spirituality.

Today, our society needs the guidance of the friends of Allah more than ever. It is in need of the guidance of scholars who have inherited the Messenger of Allah's (pbuh) knowledge, wisdom and mission of cleaning the hearts. The Iman of many has lost all conviction and is in dire need of the guidance of those stars of spirituality to bring it to life. Just as the hungry and poor people need soup kitchens, the people of spiritual hunger are longing for nourishment from the friends of Allah. Just as patients need doctors, humanity, who suffers from spiritual neglect, needs the doctors of the heart...

We have been writing articles for a long time in our Altınoluk Magazine with the title "Wisdom from Friends of Allah" in order to alleviate some of this spiritual longing. In these articles, we endeavor to remold hearts with the advice and warning of the friends of Allah. Our aim is for our spiritual world to become a clear mirror that reflects the beauty of "their universe", and our state and behavior to become blessed with the virtues of the friends of Allah.

**Dear readers!**

As you know, we started presenting you our Altınoluk articles, where we strive to explain the wise words of the friends of Allah as individual booklets for each friend of Allah. This humble work in which we have compiled our articles related to Jafar As-Sadiq is a continuation of this series.

May our Lord let us benefit from the wise advice of this great Imam of the blessed household who is inviting us to his spiritual way.

Amin!..

Osman Nuri TOPBAŞ
September, 2015
Üsküdar

# *Jafar as-Sadiq*

(May Allah have mercy on him)

# Jafar As-Sadiq رحمه الله [699 - 765]

Jafar As-Sadiq (May Allah's mercy be upon him) was born in the 80th year of the Hijrah in the Enlightened City of Madina. He was called Sadiq as he was true to his word and was extremely honest and reliable. He was also known as Sâbir (patient), Fâzıl (virtuous), Tahir (pure) and Âtir (fragrant).

Jafar As-Sadiq's father was Muhammad al-Baqir (mbuh), his grandfather was Ali Zayn al-Abidin (mbuh) and the father of his grandfather was Husayn, may Allah be pleased with him. The lineage of Jafar As-Sadiq reaches Ali from the father's side and Abu Bakr through two branches from the mother's side. Thus, by combining in his person the blessed genetics of the household of the Prophet and of Abu Bakr As-Siddiq, may Allah be pleased with him; bringing a distinct beauty to the "Golden Chain" which is a branch of the perfect guides from the age of prosperity up to the present day.

Jafar As-Sadiq grew up in a family and environment of learning, worship, virtue and morality. He learned Islamic sciences such as aqida, tafsir, hadith and fiqh from Companions such as Anas Ibn Malik, Sahl Ibn Saud and such famous Tâbiin scholars as Ata, Zuhri, Urwah, Ikrima and Nafi. In particular, he benefited a lot from his esteemed grandfathers Zayn al-Abidin and Qasim Ibn Muhammad, who were great scholars, and his venerable father Muhammad Baqir. He narrated many hadiths from them.[1] All of these men were among the great scholars and Imams of the Illuminated City of Madinah. May Allah be pleased with all of them!

In other words, both the teachers and family of Jafar As-Sadiq were people of devotion and Taqwa; they were trustworthy, just and righteous religious leaders.

Fariduddin Attar of Nishapur, began his famous work titled Tadhkiratul-Awliya, in which he compiled the lives of the friends of Allah, their exemplary stories and wise words with Jafar As-Sadiq out of respect.

---

1. For some of the hadiths that he narrated from companions such as Jabir, Ibn-i Abbas may Allah's mercy be upon them, his grandfather Kasim bin Muhammad and other Ahl-i Bayt, see. Müslim, Hac, 147-148; Ebû Dâvûd, Menâsik, 56/1905; Tirmizî, Hac 38/862, Menâkıb 20/3733; İbn-i Mâce, Mukaddime 9/65, Ticârât 41/2238; İbn-i Ebî Şeybe, Musannef, II, 115/7142; Ebû Nuaym, Hilye, III, 192, 202-203, 206; Zehebî, Siyer, VI, 255.

When Qasim Ibn Muhammad passed away, his grandson Jafar As-Sadiq was 28 years old and he had already begun transmitting the knowledge he received to people.[2]

## His Life of Worship

Jafar As-Sadiq was a great friend of Allah who chose a life of seclusion, devoting himself to learning and teaching knowledge and worship, and living in a state of servitude and submission.

Imam Malik, may Allah's mercy be upon him, states the following:

"I used to visit Jafar As-Sadiq. He always smiled and used to enjoy pleasant and humorous words. He used to tidy himself up and turn pale whenever the Prophet was mentioned.

I used to visit him for a long time. I would only ever see him in one of these three states: he either prayed, fasted or recited the Holy Qur'an.

I never saw him narrating a Hadith without being in a state of wudu (ritual purity). He would not speak about useless matters. He was one of the worshippers and devotees whose heart trembled because of the fear of Allah.

---

2. Muhammed Ebû Zehra, el-İmâmu's-Sâdık, p. 26.

When I used to visit him, he would always without fail take the cushion that he was sitting on and offer it to me…"[3]

❀

Jafar As-Sadiq, may Allah's mercy be upon him, said the followings about the prayer:

*"Prayer is closeness to Allah for every person who has Taqwa (fearful awareness of Allah). Hajj is the Jihad (struggle) of the weak. The charity of the body is fasting…*

*Make sure that your sustenance falls on you in abundance by giving Sadaqa (charity). Protect your wealth by paying Zakat (third pillar of Islam which is an obligatory annual tax on standing wealth). The one who spends out will not become poor. Caution is half of life. Being friendly with people is half of intelligence… The one who hurts his parents becomes rebellious to them. The one who cannot be patient and so behaves impulsively in times of trouble will be deprived of his reward… Allah Almighty sends patience according to the amount of misfortune and sustenance according to the amount of need. Allah opens the sustenance of those*

---

3. Kàdî Iyâz, Tertîbü'l-Medârik, II, 52; İbn-i Hacer, Tehzîbü't-Tehzîb, II, 104-105; Muhammed Ebû Zehra, el-İmâmu's-Sâdık, p. 76-77.

*who use the wealth carefully. While Allah deprives those who scatter their wealth.*"[4]

❀

Sufyan al-Thawri, may Allah's mercy be upon him, describes him as follows:

He was asked: "So why is fasting on the Eid considered reprehensible?" Jafar As-Sadiq answered by saying:

"Because people are at the feast of Allah. It is not good for a guest to fast when he has been invited to a feast."

I said: "Please let me know, why people cling to the cover of the Kaaba even though it is just a piece of cloth?" He gave me the following answer:

"It is like the person who commits a crime against someone and then clings to that person's coat and turns around for forgiveness."[5]

❀

Also, Jafar As-Sadiq stated the following in an expression of the ecstasy of worship that he had in his heart:

---

4. Ebû Nuaym, Hilye, III, 194-195; Mizzî, Tehzîbü'l-Kemâl, V, 89.
5. Zehebî, Târîhu'l-İslâm, IX, 92.

"The taste in Allah's addressing, 'O you who believe!' removes all the fatigue and heaviness of worship and prayer from the person (On the contrary, it transforms prayers to a delightful feast)."[6]

❁

Jafar As-Sadiq used to visit the cemetery at night and say:

"Oh people of the graves, why aren't you answering when I call you?"

Later, he would say to himself:

"I swear that they are prevented from answering. It is as if I became just like them now and joined them! Then he would turn towards the Qibla and be busy with contemplation and worship until the dawn.[7]

### His Good Manners

Jafar As-Sadiq was at the peak of moral virtues such as compassion, mercy, kindness, patience, forgiveness and generosity. He was not afraid of anyone but Allah. He would not fear the criticism that he faced in the path of Allah. He didn't stop doing good because of the rulers' discontent and the praise of people

6. Bursevî, Rûhu'l-Beyân, II, 185, [el-Bakara, 183].
7. Menbicî, Tesliyetü Ehli'l-Mesâib, p. 192-193

did not deceive him, nor the blame of the enemy turn him from his way.

One day, someone who lost his purse came and clung to Jafar As-Sadiq without knowing who he was, saying:

"You stole my money!" Jafar As-Sadiq asked him: "How much money was in your pouch?"

The man answered, saying:

"One thousand dinars"

Jafar As-Sadiq took him to his house and gave him one thousand dinars without saying anything. After a while the man found his pouch in his house and understood his huge mistake, so he went back to Jafar to apologize and to return his money to him. However, Jafar As-Sadiq refused to accept it, saying:

"When I give something to someone, I never take it back!" The man who was surprised by this situation, asked:

"Who is this man?" And his embarrassment was doubled when he learned that it was Jafar As-Sadiq.[8]

❁

Jafar As-Sadiq showed great submission to the judgment of God in the misfortunes he suffered. So

8. Ferîdüddîn Attâr, Tezkiretü'l-Evliyâ, p. 54; Kuşeyrî, er-Risâle, II, 384.

much so that he didn't show anything other than contentment when his little boy passed away in his arms. Tears ran down his face because of his paternal affection. However, he thought about the other blessings of Allah Almighty and said:

"You took away one blessing, but you continue to give many other blessings! If you give one trouble, you keep giving countless other blessings!" In this way he supplicated to Allah the Almighty.

Then he brought his child to his wife and other women relatives. The women started to cry out when they saw that the little baby had passed away. Jafar As-Sadiq advised them not to cry with a loud voice.

While he was going to bury his baby, he stated the following expressions coming from his heart while he was in a state of perfect resignation to the divine decree:

**"I glorify God Almighty, who took our son. We have only increased our love for Him!"**

After burying his baby, he said:

**"We are such a Community that we pray to Allah to give the things we love to those whom we love and He answers us. If He has ordained things we**

**don't like to those whom we love, we will also be pleased with that."**[9]

Here is a magnificent manifestation of the manners of servitude... As a matter of fact, one of the secrets that raises the soul to the top of spiritual knowledge is to leave aside complaints and mourning in the face of the heaviest divine tests and turn to God with an increasing submission, gratitude and love.

## His Virtues

Jafar As-Sadiq was a friend of Allah, with a smiling face and kind words. Both his outer appearance and character were radiant. He was very similar to his great grandfather Ali, may Allah ennoble his face. He was an extremely dignified and majestic man.

Jafar As-Sadiq was such a virtuous person in all aspects that many who looked at his blessed face immediately realized that he was a member of the Prophet's family.[10]

His spiritual maturity and characteristics were much higher than what can ever be expressed with words. Because of this glory he was also called "Shaykh al-Bani Hashim: The chieftain of the Hashimi Tribe".[11]

---

9. Muhammed Ebû Zehra, el-İmâmu's-Sâdık, p. 80.
10. Abu Nuaim, Hilya, III, 193; Zahabi, Siyar, VI, 257.
11. Zahabi, Siyar, VI, 255.

Remembering the following characteristics of him is enough to express his virtue:

All believers praise and send greetings to the blessed household as well as the descendants of the Prophet (pbuh) In fact, the prayer is not considered valid without sending blessings to the Prophet (pbuh) and his Ahl al-Bayt after the Tahiyyat (part of the prayer recited while kneeling) in the prayer.

❁

Jafar Ibn Muhammad was a very generous friend of Allah. He loved to feed the poor and foster the needy. Moreover, he donated so much without fearing poverty that he almost left nothing to his own family.[12]

He was similar to his respected grandfather Zayn al-Abidin in terms of secretly giving charity and curing troubles of society. During the night Zayn al-Abidin would take a bag filled with provisions such as bread, meat and money, and leave whatever was needed at the doors of the poor without anyone knowing. This was discovered only after his death, as the poor people became forlorn.[13]

They found large wounds and blisters on the back of Zayn al-Abidin while washing his blessed body.

12. Abu Nuaim, Hilya, III, 194; Zahabi, Tarih, XI, 89.
13. Abu Nuaim, Hilya, III, 136.

When the reason was investigated, it was understood that they were caused by carrying sacks of food to the poor.[14]

❁

Jafar As-Sadiq was extremely humble. One day, Sufyan al-Thawri saw precious clothes on him. When he said that these clothes don't fit the lineage of the Prophet, Jafar As-Sadiq showed the hard woolen clothes made of hair underneath. After expressing that it would be more appropriate to wear the beautiful clothes that everyone was wearing because of the financial abundance of that period that they lived in and said:

"We wore what is underneath for Allah, and the outer one for you. We have concealed what is for Allah and displayed what is for you!"[15]

Indeed, wearing old clothes in such a society could drag a person into pride and make him look like an ascetic devotee. With this behavior, Jafar As-Sadiq protected himself from hidden dangers such as hypocrisy, arrogance, pride and false modesty; and observed humility.

❁

14. Ibn Kathir al-Bidaya, IX, 112, 122.
15. Abu Nuaim, Hilya, II, 193; Zahabi, Siyar, VI, 261-262.

Jafar As-Sadiq was a man of Futuwwa, which is a term referring to the highest qualities of character that a human being should possess such as courage, serving others, generosity and self-sacrifice. One day, Shaqiq al-Balkhi asked what Futuwwa was. He replied to him by saying:

"What do you say about this matter?"

Shaqiq said:

"Futuwwa is that we give thanks when we have plenty and we are patient when we don't have."

Jafar As-Sadiq replied to him:

"Even the dogs of Madina are like this. According to us Futuwwa is to prefer for others when we have plenty and be grateful when we don't have."[16]

❀

Jafar As-Sadiq was a friend of Allah whose prayers were accepted. Whenever he asked something from Allah, that thing would be present in front of him before his prayer was over.[17] These kind of miracles are mentioned about him from various sources.[18]

16. Qushayri, Al-Risala, II, 384.
17. Abdulmajid al-Khani, al-Hadaiq, p. 129.
18. Abdulmajid al-Khani, al-Hadaiq, p. 128-129.

Because of his high virtues, some wrong beliefs, extreme exaltations and lies were invented about him even while he was still alive. He was very uncomfortable with them, he always rejected such exaltations.[19]

As a matter of fact, when Abduljabbar Ibn Abbas al-Hamadani wanted to set out from Madinah with his companions, Jafar As-Sadiq came to them and said:

"You are among the righteous ones of your city, inshallah. Let the people of your city know that I am far from anyone who claims that I am an infallible Imam whom people must necessarily obey. And I am far from whoever claims that I don't love Abu Bakr and Umar, and I have turned my face from them!"[20]

These and similar narrations support each other and all of them clearly show that Jafar As-Sadiq loved Abu Bakr and Umar (r.a). The statements attributed to the Ahl al-Bayt that they do not like Abu Bakr and Umar are nothing more than slander.

Indeed, Jafar as-Sadiq was extremely angry with the Rafizis (shia), and he would get extremely upset with them when he heard that they were secretly or

19. Muhammed Abu Zahra, Imam al-Sadiq, p. 37, 58.
20. Zahabi, Siyar, VI, 259, Tarih, IX, 90; Mizzi, Tahdhibul Kamal, V, 82.

openly speaking ill of his great grandfather Abu Bakr (r.a).[21]

## His Humility

Jafar As-Sadiq's humility was such that he didn't despise anyone and he considered each believer more valuable than himself. He called his servants and told them:

"Let's make a deal for the Judgment Day: Let's promise each other that whoever is saved on that day, will intercede to the others!"

They replied to him, saying:

"Oh grandson of Allah's Prophet! Your grandfather is the intercessor for all the worlds, how would a person like you need our intercession?!"

Jafar As-Sadiq said:

"I am ashamed to look at the blessed face of my grandfather on the Day of Judgment with these deeds and this state."[22]

❁

All scholars and devotees were striving to learn from Jafar As-Sadiq. The great friend of Allah, Dawud

21. Zahabi, Siyar, VI, 255.
22. Attar, Tazkira, p. 53.

At-Ta'i came to him one day and asked for advice by telling him that his heart was getting dark.

Jafar As-Sadiq told him:

"You are one of the greatest devotees of our age, why would you need my advice?"

Dawud At-Ta'i replied saying:

"Oh grandson of Allah's Prophet! You have superiority over people. For that it is necessary for you to advise everyone!"

Jafar As-Sadiq gave him the following magnificent answer expressing his high humility and fear of God:

"O Dawud! I am afraid that my blessed grandfather will cling to my neck and ask, "Why didn't you keep the rights of being my follower? This is not a matter that can be achieved with lineage, but only with deeds worthy of God!"

Upon this, Dawud At-Ta'i said:

"O my Lord! If someone coming from the lineage of Prophets, whose grandfather is a Prophet and mother is Batoul (Fatima, the daughter of the Prophet), lives in such a fear, who am I and how can I be happy with my deeds and behavior." And then he started crying.[23]

❁

Jafar As-Sadiq encouraged people to have humility and warned those who were selfish and arrogant. One day he came across a tribe and asked them:

"Who is your master?" One of them said:

"Me!"

Jafar As-Sadiq didn't like this answer and warned him saying:

"If you were their master, you wouldn't say "Me"! (You would say you were their servant.)"[24]

Because the ego is an obstacle in the way of being a real master.

Jafar As-Sadiq never aspired to leadership, or to be the head of people; on contrary he always preferred seclusion and silence. How can the person who dives into the oceans of Marifatullah, (direct knowledge of Allah) desire to be on the shore? The person who establishes affinity with God Almighty, doesn't value people's praises…

23. Attar, Tazkira, p. 53.
24. Abdulmajid al-Khani, al-Hadaiq, p. 132.

## His Taqwa (fearful awareness of God)

Jafar As-Sadiq, may Allah's mercy be upon him said:

"There is no better provision than Taqwa, there is nothing better than silence, there is no enemy more harmful than ignorance, there is no worse illness than lying."[25]

He would pray as follows at the end of the month of Ramadan:

"O Allah, who is the Lord of Ramadan and sent down the Qur'an! This is the month of Ramadan, in which the Qur'an was revealed, and it is about to end. O Lord, I take refuge in You the Most Generous from the rising of the sun or the departure of Ramadan without all my sins being forgiven!"[26]

❁

Imam Malik, says:

"I went on Hajj with Jafar As-Sadiq. His face changed color and he started trembling when he wanted to call Talbiyah, (prayer of the pilgrims as a conviction that they intend to perform the Hajj only for the glory of Allah). I asked him:

---

25. Abu Nuaim, Hilya, II, 196.
26. Ibn al-Jawzi, al-Tabsira, II, 103.

"What happened to you, grandson of the Prophet?"

He replied saying:

"I experienced this state when I wanted to call Talbiyah."

I asked him:

"What is stopping you from that?"

He answered:

"I am afraid of hearing from Allah something other than, 'Welcome my servant!'"'"[27]

❀

When we look at the prayers and supplications of Jafar As-Sadiq we immediately understand how great was his fear of Allah and the level of Taqwa in his heart. Thus, once he supplicated as follows:

"God! Dignify me by obeying You! Do not disgrace me by disobeying You!

God! Grant me the ability to give to those whose sustenance is constrained by You from the generous blessings that You have bestowed upon me."

The righteous people who heard this prayer said:

27. Ibn al-Jawzi, al-Tabsira, II, 142.

"This is the prayer of the Ashraf (the most honorable ones)."[28]

## His Greatness in Material and Spiritual Sciences

The blessed father and grandfathers of Jafar As-Sadiq, pursued the Companions, in order to acquire the knowledge brought by our Prophet, they learned about the Prophet's unique exemplary character, his blessed life and his Sunnah (Prophetic practice)from them. We can understand this from their narrations in the original Hadith books.

Jafar As-Sadiq grew up in a blessed family that was enthusiastic about knowledge and did not spare any effort and sacrifice for his education. He devoted himself to knowledge in Madinah, the illuminated center of learning. He wasn't content with the knowledge that he received from his family and he learned all kinds of knowledge from the Companions that had come down from the great scholars of the Tabi'un (successors of the Companions).

Later he trained great scholars in the material and spiritual sciences that he gained. Many great scholars such as Imam Malik, Sufyan al-Thawri, Sufyan Ibn Uyaynah, Abu Hanifa, Ibn Jurayj, Yahya Ibn Said and

28. Abu Nuaim, Hilya, III, 196; Mizzi, Tahdhibul Kamal, V, 91.

Yahya al-Kattan learned knowledge and narrated Hadiths from him.[29]

Jafar As-Sadiq spent his blessed life correcting the belief of people, declaring the Shari'ah and proclaiming the truth.[30]

He used to avoid politics and be more engaged in learning and teaching. He would call the scholars and jurists who did not go to the doors of the sultans for worldly interests "the custodians of the Prophets" (the Prophet's inheritors who were in the service of guiding humanity by proxy and were trusted by the Prophets).[31]

He was at the top in understanding subtle meanings and deep truths in all Islamic sciences. He was the leader of all shaykhs. Everyone trusted him. He was an ultimate guide. He was the Imam of the Muslims, the guide of the people of love and Marifatullah (direct knowledge of Allah), the reverend of devotees. He was also incomparable in his understanding of the secrets of the Qur'an and its interpretation.[32]

He was a great scholar and a faqih (expert in law) who reached the rank of mujtahid (authoritative interpreter of the law). He was a highly inspiring, truthful

29. Mustafa Öz, "Câfer es-Sâdık", DİA, VII, 1.
30. Muhammed Abu Zahra, Imam al-Sadiq, p. 63.
31. Abu Nuaim, Hilya, III, 194; Zahabi, Tarih, IX, 92.
32. See. Attar, Tadhkira, p. 51.

and reliable Imam and scholar in his ideas and narrations.[33]

All the scholars and people of his time admired his knowledge and virtue.[34]

Some of his narrations are as follows:

Jafar As-Sadiq, may Allah's mercy be upon him, transmitted this event from his father and grandfathers:

"One day, the Prophet (pbuh) took Hasan and Husain by the hand and said: 'Whoever loves me and loves these two, and their father and mother, he shall be with me on the Day of Judgment." (Tirmidhi, Manaqib, 20/3733)

❀

In another narration of Jafar As-Sadiq, the Prophet (pbuh) made this prayer:

اَللّٰهُمَّ بَارِكْ لِأُمَّتِى فِى بُكُورِهَا

"O, Allah bless deeds of my Community in the early hours of the day!" (Ibn Majah, Tijarah, 41/2238)

Jafar As-Sadiq, narrates the following Hadith with a sequence reaching to Ali:

---

33. See. Mustafa Öz, "Câfer es-Sâdık", DİA, VII, 1.
34. Zahabi, Tarih, IX, 89-90.

"O people! It is as if death was written to someone other than us! As if the truth was obligatory to someone other than us! It is as if the dead we see off will return to us after a short while! And we spend their inheritance as if we will remain forever after them. We forgot all the advice. We have started to feel safe from all misfortunes.

How happy is the one who keeps busy with his own faults and is not occupied with the faults of others! How happy is the one whose income is halal, whose inner world is clean, whose external appearance is beautiful and whose path is straight (living properly)! How happy is the one who flawlessly demonstrates modesty for Allah, who gives charity from his wealth, who sits with people of fiqh and wisdom, and helps the weak and poor! How happy is the one who gives from the surplus of his wealth and holds the excess of his words, and does not return to bid'ah (reprehensible innovation) by completely embracing the Sunnah (Prophetic tradition)."

The Messenger of Allah descended from the mimbar after saying these words." (Abu Nuaim, Hilya, III, 202-203)

❀

The scholars of Hadith who saw the isnad (chain of narrators) of hadiths narrated by Jafar As-Sadiq from his honorable father and blessed ancestor, said:

"If this isnad was recited and blown on a crazy man, he would immediately recover and come to his senses!" (Ibn Maja, al-Muqaddima, 9/65; Abu Nuaim, Hilya, III, 192)

This shows how much the Islamic scholars respect the Noble Prophet's pure and blessed offspring. On the other hand, it also points out the great virtue of the Prophet's lineage. Even reading their blessed names is a means of healing.

## His Comprehensive Knowledge of the Noble Qur'an

The Noble Qur'an is actually read from the heart. Whoever's heart is more devoted to Allah Almighty and His Prophet (pbuh), will be more aware of the secrets of the Qur'an. Since Jafar As-Sadiq had such a heart, he was more familiar with the subtleties of the holy verses than anyone else.

He was one of those who Allah Almighty is praising in this verse:

"Then We made Our chosen slaves inherit the Book. But some of them wrong themselves; some are ambivalent; and some outdo each other in good by Allah's permission. That is the great favour." (Fatir, 32)

He was a chosen slave of Allah and a saint who competed to advance in good deeds.[35]

35. Muhammad Abu Zahra, Al-Imam al-Sadiq, p. 63-64.

One day, Jafar As-Sadiq said:

"If a person is faced with a sad and dangerous situation and says "Rabbana!" five times with sincerity. Allah will make him safe from his fear and grant him what he desires."

When they asked him:

"How is that possible?"

He answered by saying:

"You can read the 191st and 194th verses from Surah Ali 'Imran!"[36]

His following words are enough to express his deep understanding of the Qur'an:

"Worship without repentance is deficient. As a matter of fact, Allah Almighty mentions repentance before worship in the following verse; "Who repent, who are devoted to worship…"[37]

"I am surprised at the person who does not say « مَاشَآءَ اللهُ لَا قُوَّةَ اِلَّا بِاللهِ » when he sees something that he likes in what he owns. For, Allah Almighty said; "Why, when you entered your garden, did you not say, "It is as Allah wills, there is no strength but in Allah"?

36. Al-Qurtubi, IV, 318.
37. Attar, Tadhkira, p. 56.

Though you see me with less wealth and children than you possess"... (Al-Kahf, 39)"[38]

"I am surprised at someone who doesn't say «لَا اِلٰهَ اِلَّا اَنْتَ سُبْحَانَكَ اِنّى كُنْتُ مِنَ الظَّالِمِينَ»; There is no God except You. Glory be to You! I have certainly done wrong."[39] when he is afflicted with sorrow and grief.

"I am surprised at someone who doesn't say «حَسْبُنَا اللّٰهُ وَنِعْمَ الْوَكِيلُ» when he is afraid of a group of people! For, Allah states the following:

"Those who were warned, "The people have gathered against you, so fear them," But that merely increased their Iman and they said, "Allah is enough for us and the best of Guardians." (Ali 'Imran, 173)"[40]

## His training al-Imam al-A'zam Abu Hanifa

Al-Imam al-A'zam Abu Hanifa not only had a relationship with Muhammad al-Baqir but he also had contact with his son Jafar As-Sadiq in scholarly matters. Although the two of them were the same age, the scholars considered Jafar As-Sadiq as one of Imam Abu Hanifa's masters.

Speaking of him, Abu Hanifa said:

38. Abdulmajid al-Khani, al-Hadaiq, p. 134.
39. Abdulmajid al-Khani, al-Hadaiq, p. 135.
40. Abdulmajid al-Khani, al-Hadaiq, p. 134.

"I swear that I did not see someone more knowledgeable than him."

Once Imam Abu Hanifa was asked:

"Who is the most faqih person that you've ever seen?" Thereupon, he reported the following incident.

"I have never seen anyone more faqih than Jafar Ibn Muhammad. When the Khalif Mansur invited him to Hira, he sent me a message saying:

"O Abu Hanifa! People are captivated by Jafar Ibn Muhammad. Prepare your toughest questions to ask him!"

So, I prepared forty questions for him. Later, Khalif Abu Jafar Mansur sent me a message; so I came to Hira and entered his presence.

Jafar As-Sadiq was sitting on the right side of the Khalif. When I saw the two of them, the awe-inspiring appearance of Jafar As-Sadiq caught my eye rather than the majesty of Khalif Mansur. I greeted them, the Khalif gave me permission and I sat. The Khalif turned to Jafar As-Sadiq and asked:

"O Abu Abdullah, do you know this man?"

He said: "Yes, he is Abu Hanifa."

Then the Khalif turned to me and said:

"O Abu Hanifa! Tell your issues, so we can ask them to Abu Abdullah"

I started to present the issues that I had prepared. I was asking and Jafar As-Sadiq was answering by saying:

"You say so and so this in this matter; people of Madina we say this." Sometimes he was agreeing with my opinion, sometimes he was agreeing with the opinion of the people of Madina and sometimes he was disagreeing with both views. He answered my forty questions with such details and did not leave any of them unanswered.

Aren't we saying that; "The wisest of people is the one who knows the disagreements best."? (He is a scholar who knows the scientific issues together with their disagreements in the best way.)"[41]

Abu Hanifa went to Madinah and stayed with Jafar As-sadiq for two years and learned a lot from him. He also met and discussed with Jafar As-Sadiq when he came to Iraq.

The following statement quoted from Imam Abu Hanifa indicates these meetings:

41. Zahabi, Tarikh al-Islam, IX, 89-90; Mizzi, Tahdhib al-Kamal, V, 79-80; Muhammad Abu Zahra, Abu Hanifa, p. 90.

"If it wasn't for those two years, Abu Hanifa would have perished!"[42]

In those various meetings, Jafar As-Sadiq taught Imam al-Azam important principles related to subtle wisdoms in religious commands and sensitive points where reason can be mistaken.[43]

For this reason, Abu Hanifa makes many quotations from Jafar As-Sadiq. These narrations can be found in many places in the book of Imam Abu Yusuf and Imam Muhammad named "Asar".[44]

### His Death

Jafar As-Sadiq spent his blessed life in the Noble Prophet's Enlightened Madina, the land of learning. He passed away in 148 Hijri and 765 AD.

He had only one thing in his will before his death: Prayer!.. He kept insistently advising in his last breath to pay attention to prayer just like the Messenger of Allah. He passed away after he strongly advised to keep the prayer, to perform it properly with awe and observe its principles.[45]

42. Âlûsî, Sabbü'l-Azâb alâ Men Sebbe'l-Ashâb, p. 157; Muhammed Ebû Zehra, el-İmâmu's-Sâdık, p. 37-39, 254.
43. See. Ebû Nuaym, Hilye, III, 196; Hânî, el-Hadâik, p. 130.
44. Muhammed Ebû Zehra, el-İmâmu's-Sâdık, p. 38, 253-254.
45. Muhammed Ebû Zehra, el-İmâmu's-Sâdık, p. 63-64.

He was buried in the blessed Jannatul-Baqi Cemetery, next to the graves of his father Muhammad Baqir, his grandfather Zayn al-Abidin and his grandfather's uncle Hasan may Allah be pleased with him.[46]

May Allah Almighty bless us with his intercession!

Amin…

## Some of His Wise Advice

"If you commit a sin, ask for forgiveness immediately!... Do not insist on the sin!"[47]

"A little of the following four things is considered a lot (in terms of danger): fire, enemy, poverty, disease."

❁

"Allah revealed to the world as follows:

O World! Serve those who serve me! Tire out and exhaust those who serve you!

One day, a fly landed on Khalif Mansur's face. Even though Mansur tried to get rid of it, he couldn't manage to send it away. Meanwhile, Jafar As-Sadiq came and Khalif Mansur asked him:

46. Prof. Dr. Hasan Kâmil Yılmaz, Altın Silsile, p. 48.
47. Hânî, el-Hadâik, p. 130.

"O Imam! Why did Allah Almighty create the fly?"

Jafar As-Sadiq answered him by saying:

"To disgrace the tyrants with it!"[48]

❁

When they asked Jafar As-Sadiq:

"Why did Allah prohibit usury?" He gave the following answer:

"So that people do not deprive each other of their beneficence and withhold support from each other!"[49]

❁

It is reported that Sufyan al-Thawri said the following:

"I went to Jafar As-Sadiq and said:

"O grandson of the Prophet! Please give me advice." He replied:

"O Sufyan!

- The liar does not have any generosity or courage,

- The envious never get any peace of mind

48. Ebû Nuaym, Hilye, III, 198; İbnü'l-Cevzî, Sıfatü's-Safve, I, 392.
49. Zehebî, Târîhu'l-İslâm, IX, 92.

- There is no friend for the miser,

- Do not expect brotherhood from an insensitive man,

- There is no good in someone whose moral behavior is bad."

I said: "O blessed grandson of the Prophet, please give me more advice." He replied:

"O Sufyan!

- To be a devotee, stay away from what is forbidden.

- To be a Muslim, be pleased with what Allah has given you.

- Just as you want people to be friends with you, be a sincere friend to them, then you will be a true believer.

- Do not accompany a wrongdoer so you will not be affected by his liberalism. As it is stated in the Hadith:

"A man follows the religion of his intimate friend; so each one should consider whom he makes his intimate friend."[50]

50. Ebû Dâvûd, Edeb, 16/4833.

- Consult those who have Taqwa and are afraid of Allah!"

I said to Jafar As-Sadiq again:

"O blessed grandson of the Prophet, please give me more advice." He replied:

"My father taught me three things. He told me:

- Dear son! He who is together with bad friends is not safe.

- The one who goes in and out of bad places will be implicated.

- The person who does not control his tongue will regret it!"[51]

### His Bequest for His Son

Jafar As-Sadiq, may Allah be pleased with him, presented the following wise advice to his son Musa al-Kadhim:

"My son! Accept my bequest and keep my advice! If you apply it, you will live in good fortune and be peaceful, and will die grateful.

My son! One who is satisfied with what is specified for him will be rich, but one who is always looking

51. İbn-i Hacer el-Heytemî, ez-Zevâcir, I, 28; Hânî, el-Hadâik, s.130-131.

for what is in others' hands will be greedy and die poor...

When a man belittles his faults, then he exaggerates that of others; similarly, when a man considers his faults to be very grave then he belittles the sins of others.

My Son! For the One who searches for the mistakes of others in order to disclose them, his own faults will certainly be disclosed.

The person who carries the sword of cruelty, will one day be killed with it, just as the one, who digs a hole for his brother will eventually fall in it.

When a man interacts with fools, he loses his honor. On the contrary, when a man interacts with scholars, he becomes a respected person.

My son! Be careful of scorning people as they will scorn you in return. Beware of interfering in something that doesn't concern you, otherwise you will be disgraced because of it!

My son! Tell the truth whether it is in your favor or against you, as this will make you respected in society.

My son! Recite the Book of Allah; spread the greeting; command the good; forbid the bad; visit those who don't visit you; take the first step to speak with the one who doesn't speak with you and give to the person who asks from you!

Be careful about gossiping as it plants the seeds of hatred in the hearts of people; beware of searching for the faults of people, as the one who reveals people's faults becomes their target…

My son! If you are going to visit someone, visit the righteous people! Do not visit sinners! Because they are like a solid rock deprived of water, a dry tree without leaves, and a barren land without grass."

Musa Kadhim followed his father's bequest and applied it until he passed away.[52]

52. Ebû Nuaym, Hilye, III, 195-196; İsmâil bin Muhammed, Siyeru's-Selefi's-Sâlihîn, p. 723-724.

# Jafar as-Sadiq

(May Allah have mercy on him)

1

A true believer considers the Divine decree more valuable than his own desires. He always welcomes the tests that come from God with gratitude and contentment. Truly Allah Almighty is pleased with the one who reaches this state of contentment and gives him these good tidings:

"O self at rest and at peace, return to your Lord, well-pleasing and well-pleased! Enter among My slaves! Enter My Garden." (Al-Fajr, 27-30)

# Jafar As-Sadiq رحمه الله -1-

Jafar As-Sadiq said:

"Allah Almighty has hidden three things in three matters:

1. His pleasure in His obedience. So, do not underestimate any act of obedience, as His pleasure might be hidden in it.

2. His wrath in His disobedience. So, do not underestimate any act of disobedience, as His wrath might be hidden in it.

3. His friends among His creatures. So, do not underestimate any believer, as intimate friendship with Allah might be hidden in him.[53]

Then Jafar As-Sadiq added:

"Allah almighty hid the acceptance of the dua (supplication) among the duas made to Him. So do

53. Ebû Tâlip Mekkî, Kutü'l-Kulûb, I, 347; Gazâlî, İhyâ, IV, 49.

not stop making dua; as His acceptance might be hidden in one of them."[54]

[The pleasure of God Almighty is sometimes hidden in a big, sometimes a medium and sometimes a small thing. In this respect, believers should consider all righteous deeds as opportunities that should not be missed, regardless of whether they are big or small.

Abu Bakr, may Allah be pleased with him, used to milk the sheep of the orphan girls around him and meet their needs before he became Khalif. People thought that he would not be able to deal with such seemingly small matters after he becoming Khalif. However, he continued this service, which he considered as a great blessing for himself, with the same humble attitude.[55]

For, only Allah Almighty knows which righteous deeds are the most valuable and of most benefit to His servants. On the other hand; the wrath of Allah can sometimes manifest in great, sometimes medium and sometimes small sins. Even the smallest sins are as heavy as mountains for the devout servants who are aware of this reality. However, even the heaviest sins seem light like a sweet melody to the heedless ones.

---

54. Gazâlî, İhyâ, IV, 49.
55. See. Süyûtî, Târîhu'l-Hulefâ, p. 80; Sarıçam, Hz. Ebû Bekir, p. 82.

Abdullah Ibn Masud, may Allah be pleased with him, from the Companions says:

*"Verily, the believer views his sins as if he were sitting under a mountain, fearing it will fall on him. The deviant views his sins as if they were a fly passing over his nose."* (al-Bukhari, Dawat, 4; Muslim, Tawba, 3)

In this respect, a believer should pay the necessary attention to all his actions, regardless of whether they are big or small, in terms of sins or good actions, and he should always take into account that they are a divine test. He should evaluate all matters with the foresight of his Iman and serve God with a sensitive heart at all times.

In this sense, he should never forget the principle of "considering everyone you see as Khidr and every night as Laylatul-Qadir." Because no one truly knows the value of a servant in the sight of Allah. Allah has attached superiority to the virtue of "Taqwa" (piety). And taqwa is in the heart. The windows of the heart are open only to Allah. Since it is not possible to know what is in the hearts of people, we can't completely know who is superior in the sight of Allah.

In this respect, despising the servants of Allah indirectly means to see oneself as superior, which is definitely incompatible with the morality of Islam. God Almighty warns His servants about this state as follows:

**"Woe to every faultfinding backbiter!"** (Al-Humazah, 1)

The following statements of the Noble Prophet (pbuh) are also an important measure regarding this issue:

*"How many are there with disheveled hair, covered with dust, possessing two cloths, whom no one pays any notice to - if he swears by Allah then He shall fulfill it."* (Tirmidhi, Manaqib, 54/3854)

*"Shall I not tell you about the inhabitants of Paradise? They are weak and nobody cares about them as they are not paid any heed because of their weakness. If they swear an oath by Allah, Allah fulfills it..."* (Bukhari, Ayman 9, Tafsir 68/1, Adab 61; Muslim, Jannat, 47)

That is to say, the duty of a Muslim is to think positively about Allah's servants regardless of who they are; to be decent and to treat them well.

On the other hand, we should continue with all supplications, especially those stated in the Qur'an and Sunnah, as much as we can. For, it is also unknown which supplication will be the means of our salvation or through whose supplication we will attain the divine mercy.]

When they asked Jafar As-Sadiq:

"What happened to us, we are praying but our prayers are not accepted? He answered them saying:

"Because you are making supplication to someone that you don't know!"[56]

[The believer begins to receive shares of marifatullah as he contemplates the might of his Lord. Marifatullah means to know Allah by direct experience and witnessing not just by a report. The level of acceptance of worship in the divine presence is according to the servant's share of marifatullah.

As stated in the following verse:

**"Are those who know equal to those who do not know?"** (Az-Zumar, 9) What is meant by the expression "to know" here is to know Allah, that is Marifatullah.

In addition, the more a servant knows his Lord, the more he increases his prayers and supplications. The servant's sincerity is the basis of his closeness to his Lord and his value in the sight of God.

As we find stated in another verse:

**"Say, "What has My Lord to do with you if you do not call on Him?"** (Al-Furqan, 77)

That is why the devout believers always live in a state of supplication during both good and bad times

56. Kuşeyrî, er-Risâle, II, 424-425; Hânî, el-Hadâik, p. 130.

of life. Staying away from supplication is a sign of distance from Allah. In fact, the inability to know Allah Almighty properly lies under the root of all sins and rebellions.

As, Qasim Ibn Muhammad, may Allah's mercy be upon him, warned someone who said:

"How bold is so and so against Allah!" and said:

"Being bold against Allah, is beyond the limits of the sons of Adam! Instead of that, say:

"How little he knows Allah!"[57]

Therefore, a believer who knows Allah Almighty takes refuge in Him in a state of nothingness, neediness and weakness, as a necessary act of servanthood.

Hasan al-Basri said:

*"I am not afraid that your prayers will not be accepted. I am afraid that you will become unable to pray..."*

Abandoning supplications with the thought that your prayers and supplications will not be accepted means falling into one of the traps of Shaytan (satan). The believer should never let go of his weapon of prayer against Shaytan, who is his open enemy and he

57. İbn-i Asâkir, Târîhu Dımaşk, c. 49, p. 180.

should never abandon his sincere prayers overflowing from his heart.

Supplication is an important act of worship as it is an order from our Lord. Our Noble Prophet (pbuh) said in a Hadith:

*"There is nothing more precious than supplication in the sight of Allah. Supplication is the essence of worship (servanthood)."* (Tirmidhi, Dawat, 1)

*"Whoever wants his supplications to be accepted in times of trouble and hardship, should make supplication abundantly in times of abundance and comfort."* (Tirmidhi, Dawat, 9)

*"Whoever among you has the door of supplication opened for him, the door of mercy is opened for him as well."* (Tirmidhi, Dawat, 101)

*"Supplicate to God when you are assured of being answered, and know that God does not answer a supplication which comes from a careless and inattentive heart."* (Tirmidhi, Dawat, 65)

In this respect, supplications - whether accepted or not - benefit the believer in any case. For, some supplications are accepted and they become a means for the servant to attain what he desires while he is still alive. While, some supplications are not answered in this world and their fulfillment is postponed to the hereafter. The wisdom behind this is to permit the servant to receive its reward in the hereafter. Zayd Ibn Aslam used to say:

*"No-one makes a supplication without one of three things happening. Either it is answered, or it is stored up for him, or wrong actions are wiped out by it."* (Muwatta, Qur'an, 36)

Moreover, it is stated in the Qur'anic Verses as follows:

**"If My slaves ask you about Me, I am near. I answer the call of the caller when he calls on Me."** (al-Baqarah, 186)

*"Your Lord says, "Call on Me and I will answer you. Those who are too proud to worship Me will enter Hell abject."* (al-Mu'min, 60)

In short, the duty of a believer is to hold on tight to the prayer by obeying the order his Lord. In particular, not to let the dawn pass by, which is the closest time to acceptance, without praying, asking forgiveness and doing dhikr (remembrance).]

Jafar As-Sadiq said:

"The best of servants is the one who gathers these five virtues in himself:

1. He is happy when he does something good.
2. He repents when he makes a mistake.

3. He is grateful when he is given blessings.

4. He is patient when he is subjected to troubles.

5. He forgives when he is wronged."[58]

[Jafar As-Sadiq draws attention to the distinctive qualities of a perfect believer with this wise advice. According to this, a believer feels an inexpressible taste in doing good and he considers the righteous deeds as a means of peace. On the other hand, he repents immediately when he falls into a mistake and never insists on his mistake. On the contrary, he knows that insisting on a mistake is an evil habit. Therefore, he tries to compensate for his mistake with sincere regret.

The way to compensate for this is stated in the following Hadith:

*"Fear Allah wherever you are. Do good immediately after a wrong action to erase it, and always be well-mannered in your relationship with people!"* (Tirmidhi, Birr, 55/1987)

A true believer sees the opinion of his Lord about himself more valuable than his own desires. He always welcomes the bitter and sweet manifestations of test that come from God with a state of gratitude and consent. In fact, this is the first condition of a peaceful heart.

58. İbn-i Şemsü'l-Hilâfe, el-Âdâbü'n-Nâfia, p. 14.

The Messenger of Allah (may Allah bless him and grant him peace) states the following about this quality of a believer:

*"How wondrous is the affair of the believer? There is good for him in every matter and this is not the case with anyone except the believer. If he is happy, then he thanks Allah and thus there is good for him, and if he is harmed, then he shows patience and thus there is good for him."* (Muslim, Zuhd, 64)

In other words, the believer must strive to gain benefit from all circumstances that he encounters in the tests of life. For this reason, he should tolerate the mistakes and faults that occur and try to be worthy of divine forgiveness by forgiving Allah's servants.]

Jafar As-Sadiq said:

"Good deeds can only be accomplished with the following three things:

1. Performing it immediately when the decision is made without any negligence.

2. Underestimating the deeds performed and staying away from vain feelings.

3. Performing it secretly in order to avoid showing off!"[59]

59. Ebû Nuaym, Hilye, III, 198.

[It is necessary to hurry to good deeds. For, if one acts slowly and negligently in an issue that Allah has commanded, many obstacles may emerge. The ego and Shaytan will also try to discourage the servant from it. If they cannot derail him from the good action then they try to empty it and make him lose the reward by violating it with selfish goals such as vanity, arrogance and complacency.

The greatest enemies of righteous deeds are pride, arrogance and vanity. We must hide good deeds in order to avoid these destructive qualities. It is necessary to protect the sincerity of the heart in the good deeds that are performed openly. In addition, considering good deeds as insufficient and little regardless of how great they are is a virtue that protects the heart from pride, arrogance and vanity.

The knowledgeable people say "forget two things":

1. Forget your good deeds, so that they do not give you pride, arrogance and vanity.

2. Forget the evil done to you so that seeds of anger and hatred do not grow in your heart.

On the other hand, they said "do not forget two things":

1. Do not forget the mistakes and faults that you have made so that you may be preoccupied with re-

pentance and compensation in order to prevent your ego from vanity.

2. Do not forget the favors done to you so that you may not be ungrateful.

In short, it is necessary for the servant to carefully protect his good deeds so that he doesn't lose his most precious provisions in his eternal journey. He must observe the principle of sincerity with great care. Otherwise, he will empty his bag that he is trying to fill and will arrive at the divine presence empty-handed.

Jafar As-Sadiq said:

"Friendship is only possible with certain conditions. If someone possesses one or some of the following qualities, it means he can be a true friend:

✓ The first measure of friendship is; being sincere with you, without expecting anything in return.

✓ The second one is that he should consider your difficult situation as his own trouble and your goodness as his own welfare.

✓ The third one is that he should not change his state according to your wealth and position.

✓ The fourth one is that he should not spare anything that he has in his capacity.

✓ The fifth one embraces all the above qualities; and that is he should not leave you in times of trouble."[60]

[In this time, most people are friends for their own interests. In this respect, we should not be deceived by the friendship claims of people who are unable to pass the tests of friendship.

In this regard, the following measures of Umar, may Allah be pleased with him, should not be forgotten:

"Do not let the prayer of a man deceive you nor his fasting.

✓ Rather, look at the truthfulness of his speech,

✓ His trustworthiness whenever he is entrusted,

✓ And how he acts whenever he is given wealth and power."[61]

Also, someone was praising someone else in the presence of Umar Ibn al-Khattab, Umar told him:

"Have you ever traveled with him?" He answered:

"No."

"Have you ever done business or any social transaction with him?"

60. Safedî, el-Vâfî bi'l-Vefeyât, Beyrut 1420, XI, 100.

61. Beyhakî, es-Sünenü'l-Kübrâ, VI, 288; Şuab, IV, 230, 326.

"No."

"Have you ever been a neighbor to him?"

"No."

Upon these answers, Umar said to him:

"I swear by Allah, except from whom there is no God that you don't know him."[62]

That is to say, it is necessary not to make a judgment about a person without testing him until he reveals his real identity. This issue is extremely important in choosing friends.

The person who has a true friend that will love, warn, protect and support him for the sake of Allah in his difficult times, has the most precious wealth in the world.

A true friend brings "ease, not trouble", in other words, he is not a burden to his friend, on the contrary he lightens his burden.

A true friend is like the stars, he appears only when darkness falls. He enlightens his friend's dark day -to the extent of his strength and capacity-, and he is concerned with his troubles.

In this respect, tea and coffee chitchats in times of ease should not be considered enough to know true

62. Gazâlî, İhyâu Ulûmi'd-Dîn, Beyrut 1990, III, 312.

friendship. Real friendship is the friendship of hard times.

As it is extremely difficult to find a true friend, the believer should first try to become a true friend to others and increase the number of these kinds of friends by being a living example.]

Jafar As-Sadiq explains the reality of "Isti'adha", which is "أَعُوذُ بِاللهِ مِنَ الشَّيْطَانِ الرَّجِيمِ: I seek refuge in Allah from Shaytan, the expelled" by saying:

"Isti'adha means cleaning the mouth from lies, backbiting and slander to honor the recitation of the Qur'an."[63]

[Just as the believer washes his mouth while making Wudu (ritual washing in preparation for the obligatory prayer) and makes an apparent cleaning before the recitation of Qur'an and the remembrance(dhikr) of Allah Almighty, he must also subject his heart to a spiritual cleansing by washing his heart with repentance, asking for forgiveness by shedding tears; from the dirtiness of lies, backbiting, slandering and similar sins. For, the real recitation of the Qur'an is performed with the heart. As there are no complete benefits and spirituality gained from the Qur'an that is not recited with a clean heart.

63. Bursevî, Rûhu'l-Beyân, X, 515, [en-Nahl, 100].

How exemplary is the following remark of our mother Aisha, may Allah be pleased from her:

"Strangely enough, a person washes his mouth not because of the ugly word he made about his Muslim brother, but because of the halal food he ate!"[64]

Indeed, there is no point in cleaning and decorating the body and the external appearance when the heart is contaminated with ugly habits. In fact, the inscription in an old Turkish bath in Istanbul contains the following parable:

Meaning, "If you are a bad mannered person with corrupt character, do not expect anything from the bathhouse! If you want a complete cleansing, first wash your heart and then your body!"

One day, Ibrahim Ibn Adham, who is one of the great saints, washed the smelly and dirty mouth of a sleeping drunkard. When they asked him why he did so, he gave the following answer:

"It would be disrespectful if I left the tongue and mouth dirty since it is created to mention the Almighty God..."

When the drunk man woke up, they told him that:

64. Ahmed bin Hanbel, ez-Zühd, I, 59.

"The devotee of Khorasan, Ibrahim Ibn Adham washed your mouth..." The heart of the drunkard, who was embarrassed by this situation, was awakened to the truth and he said:

"Then, I will repent now..."

Ibrahim Ibn Adham, who inspired this repentance, received a divine call in his dream, saying:

"You washed his mouth for Us; and we washed his heart for you!."]

May Allah Almighty enable all of us to reach an inner and outer cleansing. May He let us live a life of servitude and come to His divine presence with a Qalbi-Salim, in other words, with a spiritually purified heart.

Amin!

WISDOM FROM THE FRIENDS OF ALLAH

# *Jafar as-Sadiq* 2

(May Allah have mercy on him)

"There are four things which are a virtue as well as an obligation:

1. Sitting with the righteous is a virtue while obeying them is an obligation.
2. Reciting the Qur'an is a virtue and acting according to it is an obligation.
3. Visiting graves is a virtue and preparing for your grave is an obligation.
4. Visiting patients is a virtue and taking lessons from them is an obligation.

(İbn-i Hacer, Münebbihât, p. 14)

# Jafar As-Sadiq رحمه الله -2-

Jafar As-Sadiq said:

“Avoid being friends with five kinds of people!

1. The liar: Because you will fall into delusion as long as you are with him. He is like a mirage. He will show you what is far as near and what is near as far.

2. The fool: He will hurt you when he wants to be useful, without realizing it.

3. The stingy: He will withhold what you need the most.

4. The coward: He will surrender you to others and run away in difficult times.

5. The wicked: He will sell you out for a bite of food or even less.”[65]

[It is stated in a Hadith that:

65. Gazâlî, İhyâ, II, 172.

*"A man follows the religion of his intimate friend; so, each one should consider who he takes as his intimate friend!"* (Abu Dawud, Adab, 16/4833)

No person can choose his parents or the environment in which he is born. However, it is up to a man to choose who he will be friends with, and he is responsible for these choices. For, man takes shares from the state and manners of his friend and builds his personality and character due to these influences. Most of the time he turns to the right or the wrong path due to the influence of his friends. Therefore, being intimate and establishing friendship with people that are morally corrupt is not different from inviting poison into your spiritual life.

Jafar As-Sadiq drew attention to this reality and suggested staying away from people who have various spiritual and moral deviations, except for warning them and giving them advice. For, bad habits and egotistic diseases spread easily through friendship and this can drag a person down and weaken his Iman.

The most dangerous one of these is the "lie". As it is stated in a Hadith:

*"Truthfulness leads to righteousness, and righteousness leads to Paradise. And a man keeps on telling the truth until he becomes a truthful person. Falsehood leads to Al-Fajur (i.e. wickedness, evil-doing), and Al-*

*Fajur leads to the Fire, and a man may keep on telling lies till he is written as a liar."* (Bukhari, Adab, 69)

Truthfulness is so important that it is stated as follows while mentioning the Day of Reckoning in this holy verse:

**"...This is the Day when the sincerity of the sincere will benefit them."** (Al-Ma'idah, 119)

Truthfulness is an integral characteristic of a Muslim. Even unbelievers used to call the Noble Prophet (pbuh) before his Prophethood with "al-Amin" (trustworthy) and "as-Sadiq"(loyal) instead of addressing him by his name. As trustworthiness and loyalty are intrinsic to his nature.

Again, one day they asked the Prophet (pbuh):

"Can the believer be a coward?"

He said, "Yes." He was asked,

"Can the believer be a miser?"

He said, "Yes." He was asked,

"Can the believer be a liar?"

The Prophet (pbuh) said, "No, never!" (Muwatta, Kalam, 19; Bayhaqi, Shu'ab, IV, 207)

A believer stays away from lying and never gives up being truthful and honest, even if he cannot avoid mistakes and faults due to being human, even if he knows that it is against him in his worldly plan.

It is known that the Prophet (pbuh) never used an expression that is not true even when joking. His sensitivity about truthfulness reached such a level that when a woman called her child, saying:

"Come here and I shall give you something. The Messenger of Allah (pbuh) asked her, "What did you intend to give him?" She replied, "I intended to give him some dates. The Messenger of Allah (pbuh) said,

*"If you were not intending to give him anything, a lie would be recorded against you."* (Abu Dawud, Adab, 80/4991; Ahmad, II, 447)

We should never forget that ugly characteristics such as breaking promises, tricking and deceiving, not only spoil one's morality, but also undermine Iman.

As it is stated in a Hadith:

*"He who is not trustworthy has no Iman."* (Ahmad, III, 135)

The mother of the believers, Aisha, may Allah be pleased with her, said the following to indicate the immense harm that lies have:

"There was no behavior more hated to the Messenger of Allah than lying. A man would lie in narrating something in the presence of the Prophet, and he would not be content until he knew that he had repented." (Ibn Sa'd, I, 378)

Another meaning of the word "Mu'min", which is the common name of those who believe and trust in Allah, is a person who inculcates trust and safety to his environment. In this respect, as believers, we should not forget that we are in the Community of the Prophet who is known as "al-Amin" (trustworthy) and "As-Sadiq" (truthful or loyal) even before his mission of Prophethood, and we should try to take on his manners as our example as much as we can.

As the Noble Prophet (pbuh) said:

*"A person will be with those whom he loves."* (Bukhari, Adab, 96)

This togetherness is not only about the apparent; but it is the union of state, deeds and manners. For this reason, we should not forget that we are today's representatives of the Prophetic manners, and we should try as much as we can to always have a character worthy of Islamic moral perfection.

For this, we should not neglect following the principles of honesty and truthfulness, and we should pay attention to choosing our friends from such people.

Secondly, those whom Jafar As-Sadiq advised to avoid friendship with were "fools". As, the fool will harm his friend while he thinks he is benefiting him without being aware of it. In other words, he is the heedless person who is concerned with reviving other hearts without knowing that his own heart is dead. Just like the following story narrated by Mawlana Rumi:

One day, someone became a Companion to Jesus (pbuh). This man saw some bones in a corner while they were travelling and said to Jesus (pbuh):

"O Jesus! Please teach me the supreme name (Ismal-Adham) so that I may revive those bones and bring them to life."

Jesus replied to him:

"That is out of your capacity. You need to have a breath cleaner than the rain and be more receptive than the angels in terms of servanthood in order to resurrect the dead by reciting the Ism al-Adham. The Ism al-Adham needs a clean mouth (from illegal and doubtful food) and a heart purified from everything that distracts from Allah. That is, such a person who is not contaminated with haram and free of disobedience. A person's prayer is not acceptable unless his ego is purified!

For example, let us suppose that you have the staff of Prophet Moses. Do you have the power of Moses to transform that staff to a snake? Accordingly, what's the use for you in reciting the Ism al-Adham if you don't have the breath of Jesus?"

However, the heedless man did not stop there and he said:

"O Jesus! If I don't have that capability, at least you can recite on these bones!" Jesus (pbuh) was surprised by this foolish man and said:

"O Lord! What is the wisdom behind this? Why is this foolish man so inclined to discuss? His heart is dead, but he is trying to resurrect someone else's body when his duty is to try to revive his own heart. Instead of praying to revive his own heart, he is trying to revive others. What terrible heedlessness is this!"

Najmaddin Kubra, who is one of the great saints, attended a righteous one's funeral with his students. Najmaddin Kubra smiled during the talkin (reminding the dead how to answer the angels' questions). The students, who were surprised by the sudden smile of their teacher, asked the wisdom behind it. He didn't want to explain at first, but he said the followings after they insisted:

"The living one advises and reminds the dead how to answer angels' questions. However, the heart of the adviser is dead while the dead man's heart is completely alive. I was surprised by the heedless who advises the one whose heart is alive."

The greatest foolishness in life is observing the flawless creation of Allah with a dull and long face far from being able to understand and reflect on the wisdom behind it.

Again, the worst foolishness is to remain unaware of the wisdom behind the manifested divine power and majesty, which is displayed in the universe. It is as if many consider themselves free and irresponsible like a stray animal - falling into the simplicity of explaining life and the universe as a meaningless coincidence, despite the divine order that presents a degree of perfection and magnificence which dazzles the mind. God Almighty says the following about such people:

**"...They have hearts they do not understand with. They have eyes they do not see with. They have ears they do not hear with. Such people are like cattle. No, they are even further astray! They are the unaware."** (Al-A'raf, 179)

These are blind hearts that refuse to acknowledge the radiant light of the midday sun and cover their eyes with their hands, choosing to disbelieve. For, the desire to satisfy their selfish passions blinded their hearts and turned them into dark dungeons. Because of this reason, the fool avoids contemplating vital questions like; "Who created this universe, in whose kingdom are we living, why did we come to this world, where are we going?..". But this denial cannot save them from facing the truth that they were trying to escape from.

The worst foolishness is to seek the truth where it can never be found. In other words, trying to find happiness in the bazaar of misery and getting tired in vain. Just like rats that search for food in the sewer.

Again, the worst foolishness is the fanaticism of seeing oneself as the only representative of truth even though the person is stuck in the bog of falsehood. It is being a toy in the hands of the ego and Shaytan (satan) by relying only on the limited mind in the drunkenness of arrogance, pride and self-centeredness.

The saddest and most widespread foolishness is to prefer this temporal world to the eternal next world, being deceived by the lower desires and worldly delights. It is to take a drop of water and sacrifice the ocean for its sake or to sell the unlimited in order to gain something limited. As Umar, may Allah be pleased with him, said:

"It is to destroy one's hereafter in order to prosper in the world of others." In other words, it is to lose the pleasure and eternal reward of the generous Lord due to the distraction of fleeting enjoyment.

Friendship with those who are caught in such a flood of heedlessness and foolishness does not benefit.

For this reason, it is essential to carefully avoid the friendship of the fool.

Thirdly, the people who Jafar As-Sadiq advises us to avoid friendship with are the "stingy".

We shouldn't forget that wealth has two major enemies. One is "extravagance" and the other is "stinginess". Extravagance is an ego show of power to suppress the feeling of inferiority. While stinginess is from the cowardice of relying on one's own wealth instead of relying on Allah.

Allah Almighty states that His righteous servants, whom He is pleased with, stay away from these two ugly extremes, by saying:

**"Those who, when they spend, are neither extravagant nor mean, but take a stance mid way between the two."** (Al-Furqan, 67)

As stated before, the main characteristic of the stingy person is "cowardice". As stated in the verse:

**"Shaytan promises you poverty and orders you to avarice** (greed or stinginess)**..."** (al-Baqara, 268)

The stingy one tries to save more than he needs due to his lack of trust in the divine order of provision, and he always trusts his own wealth. The reality is emphasized as follows in Surah al-Humazah:

"(Woe to) **who has amassed wealth and hoarded it! He thinks his wealth will make him live forever. No indeed! He will be flung into the Shatterer. And what will convey to you what the Shatterer is? The kindled Fire of Allah reaching right into the heart."** (Al-Humazah, 2-7)

The stingy man or women who considers their wealth the guarantee of their existence, would not hesitate to abandon their friends from fear of losing his wealth. In other words, they prefer losing friends than losing wealth. Tightfisted people are deprived of high virtues such as loyalty, compassion, rightfulness and sincerity which cannot be bought with money.

Bad manners and ugly characteristics are always interdependent. The stingy person is merciless, the merciless person is proud and arrogant, and the arrogant person is far from being devoted in the way of Allah. Which means, stinginess is an ugly quality that is connected to all manner of bad traits and ultimately leads to moral destruction.

As it is stated in a Hadith:

*"...Stinginess is the tree of hell; a stingy person holds on to its branches and these will surely take him to hell!"* (Bayhaqi, Shuab ul-Iman, VII, 435)

Therefore, it is necessary to stay away from stingy people and approach their offers of friendship with caution.

The fourth type of people that Jafar As-Sadiq advises us to avoid friendship with are "cowards". Because the coward is a person of low character who flees and surrenders his friend to his enemy when he faces difficulties. These kinds of ugly traits are neither compatible with Islamic morality nor with the law of religious brotherhood…

As a matter of fact, it is stated in a Hadith:

*"A Muslim is the brother of a Muslim, so he should not oppress him, nor should he hand him over to an oppressor…"* (Bukhari, Mazalim, 3; Muslim, Birr, 58)

A Muslim who has Iman (belief) knows that he should not fear anyone but Allah. Hence, he is saved from being the servant of other servants.

Our Prophet (pbuh), who is the example for his Ummah (Community) in every respect, took refuge in Allah from cowardice in his prayers, and encouraged his Companions by fighting in the front line against the enemy. His marvelous bravery and valor was admired and emulated by the leader of the courageous ones, Ali (mabph), who narrated one of his countless states of courage as follows:

"I remember the day of Badr, when we were seeking shelter with the Messenger of Allah (pbuh) and he was the closest to the enemy and the most courageous of the people on that day." (Ahmad, I, 86)

One of the countless examples of courage arising from the noble Companions is the incident of the blind Companion, Abdallah Ibn Umm-Maktum (mabph) who was the standard bearer in the Battle of al-Qadisiyyah.[66]

That blessed Companion wanted to join the army with an ecstatic desire to be part of the campaign. However, due to his blindness he was told not to come. It is narrated that he said the following words to those who told him that he was exempt from the battle;

"I can be of great benefit to you with this state of mine. As I am blind, I cannot see the enemy's sword, so I can carry the flag in the front line without feeling discouraged. The courage, heroism and excitement of the Muslims will increase when they see me fearlessly confronting the enemy."

What a marvelous lesson is the courage of Ibn Umm-Maktum for the healthy and strong believers.

Cowardice is a weakness that condemns people to humiliation and captivity. The manifestations of this weakness extend to the whole state and attitude of a person. For example, a coward cannot be generous. Because he is afraid that his wealth will decrease and become poor by spending money.

66. See. Kurtubî, Abese, 1-4.

Therefore, it is necessary to know that the friendship of a cowardly person will not be beneficial due to its negative and corrupting effect on the character.

Lastly, the people whom Jafar As-Sadiq advised to avoid friendship with are "sinners". The sinner is a prisoner of his ego. He has been condemned to a life of being deceived by the attraction of sins. Therefore he doesn't hesitate to betray his friend for the slightest self-interest.

It is advised to be very cautious against sinners in the following Qur'anic verse:

**"You who have faith! If a deviator comes to you with a report, scrutinize it carefully in case you attack people in ignorance and so come to greatly regret what you have done."** (Al-Hujurat, 6)

In other words, one must beware of the mischief and sedition caused by a deviant person who may appear on the side of truth but only for the sake of his selfish desires. The man of this nature is an immoral person who is desensitized to lies, slanders and insults. Hence, one cannot trust the sinner, as his words are not reliable and his testimony is not acceptable.

In addition, friendship with unbelievers causes the spread of negative states and causes gloom and darkness in the heart.

How exemplary is the following warning reported by Imam Rabbani in one of his letters:

*"Once I went to visit a sick person. He was close to death. I saw that his heart was in heavy darkness. Although I tried to lift this darkness from him, I couldn't succeed. After a lot of effort, it became clear that this darkness was caused by the negative states that have passed to him from unbelievers and the origin of this problem was his close friendship with unbelievers.*

*Later on I understood that my efforts to lift his darkness were in vain... As the cleansing of this darkness was left to the torment of hell for that is the punishment of too much close friendship with an unbeliever.*

*On the other hand, I also discovered that even a speck of belief will eventually save him from the torment of Hell. And this is the abundance of faith.*

*Then, this question came to my mind; "Is it permissible to perform the funeral prayer of this person or not?" After contemplating, I came to the clear conclusion that it would be appropriate to perform his funeral prayer. For Muslims who, despite having Faith, follow the customs of the unbelievers and observe their holy days ,it is still permissible to perform their funeral prayers. As it wouldn't be right to count them among the unbelievers. In the end, it would be appropriate to hope for their salvation from the eternal torment."* (See. Mektubât-ı İmâm-ı Rabbânî, c. I, 266. Letter)

One of the most important examples in history about the sad fate of those who become friends with the unbelievers is the Andalusian (Spain) Muslims.

Andalusians became divided and fragmented due to their egotistic passions. Moreover, the Muslim principalities established friendships with Christians to help them fight against their brothers. This friendship (!) prepared their collapse.

In short, as believers, we should be extremely careful about our friends and we must adopt this divine order very seriously, **"You who have Faith! Have Taqwa of Allah and be with the Sadiqun** (the truthful)." (at-Tawbah, 119)

Let's not forget this statement of Imam Ghazali saying that with time the physical closeness with corrupt and heedless people turns into a psychological closeness, and the psychological closeness turns into religious closeness. Step by step this drives the person into a spiritual destruction.

Allah Almighty describes a scene from the regret of people who fall into corruption and mischief with the corrupted ones in the hereafter as follows:

**"What has landed you in Saqar** (hell)?" **They will say, "We were not among those who did Salat** (prayer), **and we did not feed the poor. We plunged with those who plunged and denied the Day of Judg-**

**ment, until the Certain** (death) **came to us."** (Al-Muddaththir, 42-47)

That is to say, one of the qualities that make a servant enter to Hell, apart from not prostrating to Allah, stinginess, hard-heartedness and denying the hereafter, is to share the state of the sinners, consort with them and follow their path.

If we want to be raised up with the righteous and the faithful ones in the next world, we should stand by them in this world and emulate their states, behavior and deeds and make a great effort to follow them in terms of their worship, relationships and manners.

May Allah Almighty join us with His servants whom He loves and is pleased with.

Amin!..

WISDOM FROM THE FRIENDS OF ALLAH

# Jafar as-Sadiq

(May Allah have mercy on him)

3

Man is created from earth and he will return to earth, this cycle will continue until Judgment Day. The earth that we walk on contains both the essence/seed of all people who will come to the world and the dead bodies of billions of people who have lived… It is like billions of overlapping shadows… Tomorrow we will enter into the ground and take our place in this dense shadow. After that, an eternal life will begin…

# Jafar As-Sadiq رحمه الله -3-

Jafar As-Sadiq said:

"The person who lives according to the external form of the Holy Prophet (pbuh) is Sunni. While the one who lives according to his internal form is Sufi."[67]

[Humankind has two aspects that come from creation:

1. Turabi (earthly), which is the bodily aspect created from earth.

2. Ruhi (spiritual), which is the inner and spiritual dimension.

Just as human beings are composed of spiritual and bodily structures, the divine orders and prohibitions relate to both the external and the inner aspect of man. The body and soul, mind and heart, meaning and matter, must always be in balance and in harmo-

67. Ebû Nuaym, Hilye, I, 20

ny. Though we cannot pray without a body nor can we fast or perform any kind of good deeds without a body, the body is not the original existence of human beings. The body is just the clothing of the spirit for its journey through this world which we have to leave behind at our last breath.

If we think about it, this world is like a hotel with two doors. It has been filled with countless people who entered from one door and left from the other since Adam (pbuh) to our present day. Man is created from earth and he will return to earth, this cycle will continue until Judgment Day.

It is not our bodily strength or beauty that will benefit us in this eternal destination, but our spiritual beauty and righteous deeds.

Mawlana Rumi is gives the following advice, saying:

*"Do not prioritize overfeeding and nourishing the body! As it is a sacrifice that will be presented to the earth. Rather pay attention to feeding your heart with spiritual light. Because that is what will be honored and sublimed...*

*Feed your soul with spiritual food, like contemplation of divine wisdom, sophisticated understanding and spiritual provisions, so that it can reach its destination with full power!"*

As we have stated, the purpose of our existence in this world of tests is to return to our Lord with a pure and sound heart, by eliminating the dirt of selfish desires and ambitions. Allah sent Prophets with Divine Books and He also gave us perfect spiritual guides in order for us to achieve this.

Our Noble Lord showed the greatest favor to us by sending us His most Beloved Prophet, our master Muhammad, may Allah bless him and grant him abundant peace. He is the most exceptional wonder of the divine art ever manifested to humanity.

The Prophetic life, which is a vivid interpretation of the Qur'an, is our guide to the straight path; it is an ideal example of the "Insan Kamil" (the perfect man), and model that our Lord has shown to His servants.

Jafar As-Sadiq, may Allah be pleased with him, emphasized, that we should take the Prophet as an example not only in his external and outward aspects, but also in his spiritual, inner and moral aspects as much as we can. Otherwise, our servitude will be incomplete and inadequate like a bird that tries to fly with a single wing.

In this respect, it is essential to know the Prophet's (pbuh) spiritual sensibilities as much as knowing his words, deeds and behavior. Which means knowing the Prophet in terms of;

✓ Always preferring the hereafter,

✓ Zuhd, asceticism and doing without,

✓ His state of awe in prayer,

✓ His feelings of total submission, weakness, nothingness and deep contemplation before the manifestations of divine power,

✓ His exceptional kindness, fineness, decency and modesty with people,

✓ His immense compassion and mercy towards all creatures,

✓ His incomparable generosity, sacrifice, altruism and all his exemplary states and manners.

The essence of Sufi training is the effort of dissolving into all -external and internal- states and attitudes of the Prophet. A full observance of the Prophet's Sunnah and trying to get a share from his spirituality is necessary in order to benefit from the state and manners of the Prophet. Which means striving to understand and completely live the religion with all its aspects of the Sharia (Islamic law), Tariqa (spiritual path), Haqiqa (reality/truth) and Marifa (direct experiential knowledge). We can summarize this difference of spiritual depth in terms of understanding and living religion with the following famous example:

✓ In Shariah, it is wasteful to eat after being full.

✓ In Tariqa, it is wasteful to eat until becoming full.

✓ In Haqiqa, it is wasteful to eat anything while being unaware of the presence of Allah.

✓ In Marifa, it is wasteful to eat without witnessing the divine manifestations of the blessings. For, every being created by Allah Almighty is a proof of His might and majesty.

Sufism is the effort of engraving the spiritual sensibilities and the depth of contemplation reflected from the exemplary manners of the Prophet. Allah Almighty has sent us His most Generous Beloved Messenger and Prophet (pbuh) to all humanity until Judgment Day. Especially today, we need to understand the spiritual aspects of our Prophet with all their splendor along with his exemplary character. We all urgently need to catch a whiff of our Prophet's fragrance of mercy which pervades all creatures, whether they are Muslim or non-Muslim, animate or inanimate.

There were times when the Prophet (pbuh), who is the honor of all the worlds, tied stones over his belly out of hunger and there would be no food in his house for many days. When he attained a worldly possession, except if he had to pay a debt, he would keep nothing from it for himself, and he would give away whatever he had to the needy. This state was an incomparable pleasure for the Messenger of Allah (pbuh). He would not think about his needs and his family's necessities without meeting the needs of his Companions. In every case, he would say "my Ummah first", and he could not rest until his Community found peace.

What a beautiful example of this Prophetic sensitivity is the following event:

Once Abu Huraira (mabph) was very hungry and he tied stones over his belly, as he couldn't find anything to eat. He saw Abu Bakr (mabph) and asked him to recite a verse hoping he would feed him. Abu Bakr (mabph) answered his question and left. Later on Umar (mabph) came. He also behaved in the same way. As neither of them had the possibility to help him at that moment. Suddenly the Messenger of Allah (pbuh) saw Abu Huraira and he understood what was in his heart by looking at his face. So he invited him to his house.

They brought a small bowl of milk to the house of the Prophet. Abu Huraira was happy when he saw the milk. But the Prophet (pbuh) ordered Abu Huraira to call the Ahl al-Suffa. Ahl al-Suffa were poor Companions who were unable to earn money because they devoted themselves entirely to worship.

Abu Huraira was unpleased when the Messenger of Allah invited the Ahl al-Suffa. As the milk wasn't nearly enough for everyone.

But he immediately went and invited the Ahlal-Suffa, thinking that it wouldn't be appropriate to disobey the order of Rasulullah.

The Prophet ordered Abu Huraira to offer milk to all the Ahl al-Suffa one by one. Each of the Companions drank until he was full and gave it back. After all of the Ahl al-Suffa drank, Abu Huraira handed the bowl to the Messenger of Allah (pbuh). The Prophet gave it back to Abu Huraira and said:

"Sit and drink!" So he sat and drank until he was full. Whenever he tried to give the bowl back to the Prophet, the Prophet would repeat again and again:

"Sit and drink!"

Finally Abu Huraira (mabph) said:

"No, I swear to Allah who sent you as a messenger that there is no space left in my belly to drink more."

Eventually the Prophet (pbuh) took the bowl, he praised Allah and invoked the Name of his Lord on it and drank the remaining milk." (See. Bukhari, Rikak, 17)

The lovers of Prophet who received a share from the spirituality and generosity of the Prophet (pbuh) are the lofty souls whose hearts were transformed into a lodges of mercy. They cannot be warm while there are believers who are cold, they cannot sleep when their neighbors are hungry, they suffer from the agony of their brothers and feel responsible for the oppressed, the strangers and the orphans.

How much have our souls benefited from this spirituality? How familiar are these Prophetic sensitivities to our conscience? Do we have the spiritual vision to recognize our brothers and sisters who are going through troubles but cannot bring forward their needs due to their high levels of modesty and dignity? Do we ever say, "my brother or sister in Islam is first" instead of saying "myself first".?

Allah Almighty introduces His Beloved Prophet to us as follows:

**"A Messenger has come from among yourselves. Your suffering is distressing to him; he is deeply concerned for you; he is gentle and merciful to the Muminun** (believers)**."** (at-Tawba, 128)

In other words our Lord expresses the love and devotion of His Messenger to his Ummah with the words "rauf" (gentle) and "rahim" (merciful), which are two of His own names. For, the Prophet's affection and fondness towards his Ummah is greater than the compassion of a mother towards her child, and he showed this on numerous occasions during his blessed life.

While they were going on a campaign, he would always be on the front of the army as he wanted to be the first to face the difficulties and hardship that might come to his Ummah, and on their return, he would be at the back in order to help the wounded and grieving Muslims who were struggling and share their troubles and become a source of comfort and consolation to them.

Again, the Prophet of Mercy says:

*"I have more right than other believers to be the guardian of the believers, so if a Muslim dies while in debt, I am responsible for the repayment of his debt, and whoever leaves wealth after his death it will belong to his heirs."* (Muslim, Juma, 43; Ibn Majah, Muqaddimah, 7)

He stated that, just as he struggled for the salvation of his Ummah throughout his life, he will carry the burdens of his Ummah even after he passes away, by saying:

*"My life is good for you; you bring up new matters and new matters are brought up for you. My death, also, is good for you; your actions will be shown to me; if I see good, I shall praise Allah and if I see evil, I shall ask forgiveness of Him for you."* (Haythami, IX, 24)

*"Be careful! I am a means of safety for you in my life. And when I die, I cry out in my grave: "O Lord, my Community, my Community!..." until the first trumpet is blown..."* (Ali al-Muttaqi, Kanz al-Ummal, v. 14, p. 414)

In other words, the greatest concern of the Messenger of Allah (pbh) is the peace and eternal salvation of his Ummah. It is the duty of everyone, who has been honored by being among this Ummah, to be able to respond with the same love and affection to the Messenger of Allah, who had deep concern for his Ummah on his tongue and in his heart throughout his life.

So how is our state in this regard? How much do our desires, wishes and goals show the selfishness of saying "myself, myself", and how much do they show the futtuwa (selfless character) of saying "my Ummah, my Ummah", while our Prophet (pbuh) is praying for his Ummah in his grave until Judgment Day?

How much effort are we making to realize the desires of the Messenger of Allah (pbuh) in his prayers for his Ummah? Which of our worldly desires will we give up in order to fulfill a Prophetic desire?

To what extent are we concerned with the material needs of the Ummah of Muhammad, as well as its spiritual and religious problems?

What kind of struggle do we endeavor to do in order to try to curb the decline of religion, belief and morality?

Our Prophet (pbuh) emphasized in times of joy and sorrow, victory and defeat, abundance and scarcity that "the real life is the life of next world" and he said:

"O Allah! Do not afflict us in our religion, and do not make this world our greatest concern, nor the limit of our knowledge!..."[68]

While he is making this supplication, let us look at ourselves; do issues about our religion concern us most or just the affairs of this fleeting world?...

Among the countless worries and concerns that occupy our hearts on a day to day basis, how much do we remember the impending events of our "last breath" and our entering into the "afterlife"?...

Let us not forget that all the statements of the Prophet (pbuh) about us, his Ummah, show us a tremendous horizon of responsibility. We have to show loyalty to our "Rauf and Rahim" (kind and merciful) Prophet and be concerned with the problems of his Ummah, and strive to put a smile on his face.

Islamic scholars unanimously agree that Muslims who are able to help their oppressed brothers in any part of the world and fail to do so, are committing a very grave offense.

68. Tirmizî, Deavât, 79.

Today, the unacceptable situation of many of our people in Myanmar, Syria, Somalia, Kashmir, and other Islamic lands, is a big test for us all!

The more we are concerned with the problems of the Ummah and protect the entrustment of the Messenger of Allah, the greater the smile on his blessed face will be toward us. However -God forbid- if we are caught up in the whirlpool of envy and violate the law of brotherhood, then his gentle and graceful spirit will be hurt and be sorrowful because of us.

Indeed the Messenger of Allah (pbuh) expressed this concern, which made his heart tremble, as follows, while warning us:

"I am your predecessor before you, and I am a witness over you, and your promised place to meet me will be Al-Hawd (the basin, where the believers will drink and be refreshed on the extreme heat of the day of reckoning), and I am looking at it from this place of mine. **I am not afraid that you will worship others besides Allah, but I am afraid that the life of this world will tempt you and cause you to compete with each other for it.**" (Bukhari, Maghazi, 17; Muslim, Fadhail, 31)

Let us not forget that on the terrible Day of Judgment, we will be in need of the intercession of the Messenger of Allah (pbuh). We will desperately need to gather under his "Banner of Praise" and take refreshment from his Al-Hawd. In other words, being close to Him and being with Him is the most vital necessity.

The Sultan of the Hearts also reveals the reality of this closeness and togetherness by saying:

*"A person will be with those whom he loves."* (Bukhari, Adab, 96)

But the truth of this togetherness is a complete conformity and unity in of states, deeds, morality, feelings and ideas and a unity of direction. It is to be together with the Prophet in his fondness for his Ummah. It is to resemble him in our states of awe in worship and also to emulate him in his kindness and grace in his relations with others.

Once such a tie is established, even the furthest is considered close. But if this tie doesn't exist, even the closest is considered far away. Only those who are able to overthrow the rule of their egos and become receptive like the earth can benefit from the rain of divine mercy. However, the crude souls that are defiled by pride, arrogance and envy, are deprived of the rains of mercy just like hard rocks.

Mawlana Rumi gives us the following metaphor:

*"The sun is close both to the dry branch and the fresh branch but when the time comes, how is it possible to compare the closeness of the fresh and green branch,*

*which gives it's ripe fruit, with the closeness of the dry branch?!*

*What can a dry branch gain other than drying out even more (and becoming wood to burn) because of its proximity to the sun?!"*

Allah Almighty says in the holy verse:

**"We send down in the Qur'an that which is a healing and a mercy to the muminun, but it only increases the wrongdoers in loss."** (Al-Isra, 82)

This means that our true closeness to the Qur'an and the way of the Messenger of Allah is only in relation to our conformity in our spiritual states.

One day the Prophet said: "I long for my brothers. I missed them a lot!"

The Companions said:

"Ya Rasulullah, are we not your brothers?"

The Prophet (pbuh) said:

"You are my Companions. My brothers are those who haven't yet come to this world."

The Companions said:

"Messenger of Allah, how will you recognize those of your Ummah who have not yet been born?"

He replied by saying:

"Supposing a man had horses with white blazes on their foreheads and legs among other horses which were all black, tell me, would he not recognize his own horses?"

The Companions said:

"Certainly, O Messenger of Allah."

Thereupon, the Prophet (pbuh) said:

*"They will come with white faces and arms and legs owing to their Wudu (ablution), and I will arrive at the Hawd (basin) before them. Some people will be driven away from my Hawd as the stray camel is driven away. I will call out, 'come, come'. Then it will be said, 'these people changed the religion after you, and I will say, 'be off, be off."* (Muslim, Taharat, 39)

That is to say, the way to be together with the Prophet of Allah in the hereafter is to always be with him in this world. We should not leave his love and longing for us unrequited, and we should refresh our love and devotion to him on every occasion. Because, real love establishes a line between two hearts. A continuous "transfer of state" takes place on this line. The state and attitudes of the beloved are constantly spreading to the person who truly loves. In other words, the lover resembles the beloved according to his love, and therefore takes his share of his beloved's character. The most important spiritual education from the Messenger of Allah (pbuh) is to unite our inner world with the feelings that blossom in his heart.

Therefore, it is not sufficient to only say, 'I love the Messenger of Allah'. If we love him, how much do we follow his manners and sensitivities? How much compassion, how much affection do we have? What is the level of our morality? Are we able to say, 'the real life is the life of the hereafter'[69] when we have to choose between this world and the next? When the time comes, will we be able to renounce the self and its desires and prefer our brother to ourselves? Or are all of our expressions of love nothing but unfounded claims and lip service?!.

In this respect, it is time to review our situation regarding our loyalty to the Prophet. It is time to identify our shortcomings and take up the challenge of correcting them…]

May Allah Almighty grant us the opportunity to receive a share from the spiritual texture of our Beloved Prophet. May He adorn our hearts with his love and may our lives be saturated by following his resplendent Sunnah and may we be honored with his intercession in the hereafter.

Amin!..

69. Buhârî, Rikàk, 1.

WISDOM FROM THE FRIENDS OF ALLAH

# Jafar as-Sadiq

(May Allah have mercy on him)

4

While great efforts and fortunes are spent on children for their worldly future, to be educated in a high quality college, how much effort is made for their eternal future, that is, for their hereafter? Raising our children with authentic knowledge of Islam is the first duty of all of us. Otherwise, we shouldn't forget that our beloved children will complain about us on the Day of Judgment!.. The first duty of mothers especially is to be the teachers of their children as it is said: "اَلْاُمُّ مَدْرَسَةٌ". If the mother forgets her motherhood, the society will be filled with nests of scorpions, snakes and centipedes.

# Jafar As-Sadiq رحمه الله -4-

Jafar As-Sadiq says:

"Whoever's provision is constricted, should increase seeking for forgiveness of Allah!"[70]

Four people came to Hasan al-Basri, who was one of the friends of Allah, one of them complained about drought, the other about poverty, the other about his infertile field and the last one complained about not being able to have a child[71] and they all demanded help

70. Abdülmecid Hânî, el-Hadâiku'l-Verdiyye, sf, 161, Rehber Yayıncılık, İstanbul 1986.
71. Incidentally, let's say that sometimes people may not be able to achieve what they hope, even though they submit to Allah by praying. For example, some married couples are not able to have children although they want to very much. There are many wisdoms behind this. Because no one knows the hidden matters except Allah. Our Lord knows better what is good and what is bad for us. His appreciation for us is undoubtedly better than what we desire.
In addition, the fact that Allah withholds some blessings from

from him. That great saint recommended "Istighfar" (seeking forgiveness).

People who were around him, said:

"The troubles and distress of those people were all different, but your advice to them all was the same!"

Hasan al-Basri answered them with the following verse:

**"'Ask forgiveness of your Lord truly He is Endlessly Forgiving. He will send heaven down on you in abundant rain and reinforce you with more wealth and sons, and grant you gardens and grant you waterways."** (Nuh, 10-12)[72]

This means that Allah Almighty saves His servants, who ask forgiveness and who turn in sincere Tawba (repentance), from many troubles and gives them many blessings. Therefore, the most important

---

his servants doesn't mean that He doesn't love those servants. As we know, our Prophet's wife, Aisha (mubph) did not have any children. Allah withholds some blessings from His servants, in order to raise their rank and give them rewards that are much better and more permanent than those blessings. In this respect, it is necessary for us to always be content with the divine decree because we know that Allah only wants good for us and there are hidden blessings in things that we find bitter.

72. İbn-i Hacer, Fethü'l-Bârî, XI, 98; Aynî, Umdetü'l-Kàrî, Beyrut, XXII, 277-278.

means of attracting God's mercy and appeasing His wrath is for the servant to sincerely turn to his Lord and ask Him for forgiveness for all of his mistakes and wrong actions.

As a matter of fact, the following is stated in another verse:

**"Allah would not punish them as long as they sought forgiveness."** (Al-Anfal, 33)]

Jafar As-Sadiq said:

"Anger is the key to every evil."[73]

[The believer must be a key to goodness and a lock to evil. Anger, which is a double-edged sword, becomes the key to good when it comes from Faith, and to evil when it arises from the ego. Anger from the ego is a state that by-passes the intellect and always results in regret.

When a believer is angry for the sake of Allah, he will only be angry at that which angers Allah. He should always be careful not to let his ego get involved.

One of the best examples in this regard is the famous incident of the great Companion Ali (mabph) when he was about to kill one of the enemy in battle, then the man spat in his face and at that moment Ali

73. Gazâlî, İhyâ, III, 166.

could not go through with it and spared him. This man could not understand the odd behavior of Ali and asked in amazement and astonishment:

"O Ali! Why did you stop while you were just about to kill me? What happened so you went from violent anger to an indescribable calmness? You suddenly settled down like a calm air while you were flashing like ferocious lightning. What is the reason for this sudden change? This state of yours became a mystery to me."

Ali (mabph) gave the following answer:

"I only make jihad in the way of Allah. I strike the heads off Allah's enemies for His sake. I never involve my ego in this… You wanted to insult me, to anger me and thus to provoke my ego by spitting at my face. If I had killed you at that moment, it would have been polluted with the dirt of my ego and pride that had just been insulted. However, I do not fight for the satisfaction of my pride, but for the sake of Allah alone."

That man became a Muslim from witnessing this unparalleled virtue and self mastery of this great Companion.

Allah Almighty mentions the qualities of His righteous slaves, whom He gives the good news of divine rewards, as follows:

**"Those who give in both times of ease and hardship, those who control their rage and pardon other people – Allah loves the good-doers."** (Ali 'Imran, 134)

One of the examples of virtue that arose from the application of this verse is as follows:

Jafar As-Sadiq had a slave. He was pouring water from the pitcher while Jafar As-Sadiq was washing his hands in a basin. Suddenly the water splashed on his clothes. Jafar As-Sadiq looked at the slave with some anger. Thereupon the slave said:

"O master, it is stated in the Qur'an; "Those who swallow their anger: وَالْكَاظِمِينَ الْغَيْظَ"[74] are given the good news of Allah's forgiveness and Paradise."

Upon this, Jafar As-Sadiq said:

"Then I swallow my anger!"

The slave recited the rest of the verse:

"And those who pardon people: وَالْعَافِينَ عَنِ النَّاسِ"

Jafar As-Sadiq said:

"Ok then, I pardon you."

The slave continued reciting the verse:

"And Allah loves the good-doers: وَاللّٰهُ يُحِبُّ الْمُحْسِنِينَ"

74. Ali 'Imran, 134.

Upon this, Jafar As-Sadiq said:

"Go on, you are free for the sake of Allah! Take this thousand dinars, it is yours too!"[75]

Therefore, it is a great virtue to hold back your anger for the sake of Allah when a person faces mistakes and wrong doings. As it is stated in the Hadith Sharif:

*"The strong man is not the one who overcomes people by his strength, but the strong man is the one who controls his anger."* (Bukhari, Adab, 76; Muslim, Birr, 107, 108)

Again, the Messenger of Allah explained the way to overcome anger in personal matters as follows:

*"Behold! Anger is an ember in the heart of the son of Adam, as you see it in the redness of his eyes and the bulge of his jugular vein. So whoever senses something from that, then let him cling to the ground."* (Tirmidhi, Al-Fitan, 26/2191; Ibn Majah, Al-Fitan, 18)

*"When one of you becomes angry while standing, he should sit down. If the anger leaves him, well and good, otherwise he should lie down."* (Abu Dawud, Al-Adab, 3/4782; Ahmad, V, 152)

Abu Wa'il said:

75. İbnü'l-Cevzî, Bahru'd-Dümû', p. 142.

"We entered upon Urwah Ibn Muhammad. A man spoke to him and made him angry. So he stood up and did Wudu (ritual washing Muslims do before prayer), he then returned and said that the Messenger of Allah (pbuh) said:

*"Anger comes from Shaytan and Shaytan was created from fire, and fire is extinguished with water; so when one of you becomes angry, he should do Wudu!"* (Abu Dawud, Al-Adab, 3/4784; Ahmad; IV, 226)

However, it should be stated that it is an extremely important duty to be angry for the sake of Allah when necessary, just as important as overcoming anger when it is not necessary.

The Messenger of Allah (pbuh) was the last person who could ever get angry for his ego, nor would he argue with anyone. However, he would get angry when a right of someone else or the public was violated, and even the vein on his blessed forehead would swell, and he would not be satisfied until that right was given back and justice was restored.]

Jafar As-Sadiq said:

"Don't be sad when you hear something you don't like about yourself from your brother! If what he said is true, this upsetting word will be an expiation for a punishment that you may have had to face in the hereafter. If it is a lie, then Allah will give you a good deed without you even doing anything just because of this false word uttered about you."[76]

[What a great consolation this advice of Jafar As-Sadiq is, especially for believers who are exposed to unjust accusations. It is necessary to keep this advice in mind in order to preserve the peace of the heart.

It is a fact that no matter how good a believer is, there will always be people against him. It is in no one's power to prevent this.

As a matter of fact, the existence of ignorant and heedless people like Abu Jahl, who used ugly words against our Prophet (pbuh),goes to show that no one is safe from such slander.

Similarly, according to what Jafar As-Sadiq has reported, one day Musa (pbuh) begged Allah as follows in his supplication:

"O Lord! I want everyone to remember me well."

Allah Almighty said:

"How is that possible, I couldn't do that even for Myself."[77]

---

76. Ebû Nuaym, Hilye, III, 198.
77. Abdülmecid Hânî, el-Hadâiku'l-Verdiyye, sf, 161-162, Rehber Yayıncılık, İstanbul 1986.

In other words, no matter how good someone is, there can still be those who hate him, and subsequently set out to defame him with lies and slander.

One of the high qualities of wise believers is not to be hurt by such negative talk about them. Because, if these accusations are true, it is backbiting. If they are completely false and unjustified then it is slander. It is either a means for the wiping out of wrong actions or the elevation of the believer's rank with his Lord.

People will have to hand over their good deeds to those whom they use to backbite and gossip about on the terrifying Day of judgment, even though they themselves need them badly. If they do not have enough good deeds to offer, then they will have to bear some of the bad deeds of those whom they gossiped about.[78]

How well the following exemplary incident explains this reality:

A person who was addicted to backbiting did not hesitate to backbite a friend of Allah in his neighborhood. For this reason, no one liked that backbiter. However, whenever he came across him, that friend of Allah always greeted the backbiter with a smile and he was giving him compliments to him by saying; "Come,

78. Bkz. Buhârî, Mezâlim 10, Rikàk 48; Müslim, Birr, 59; Tirmizî, Kıyâmet, 2; Ahmed, II, 303, 324, 372.

my dear partner!". This beautiful state finally brought the backbiter to his senses, saying:

"I speak against this person here and there, but he always compliments me. I won't speak against him anymore."

So he stopped backbiting this friend of Allah. Then he stopped receiving the compliments and one day he asked why, wondering the reason behind it:

"You no longer compliment me the way you used to; your previous fondness is gone. What is the reason for this?"

The friend of Allah smiled and said:

"I used to have a commercial partnership with you. Now that partnership is over. That's why the compliments are over too." The man became surprised and said:

"What partnership? I am not aware of such a partnership." The great saint continued his explanation by saying:

"You used to speak against me here and there; and I preferred to be patient rather than responding with backbiting. As a reward for this patience, my sins were written to your book and your good deeds were written to my book. I had such a beneficial commercial partnership with you. Nowadays, you are no longer backbiting me. Which means that our partnership is over…"

The man who was astounded by what he heard, asked:

"Is this really the situation of the backbiter?"

That blessed man continued his words with the following example:

"Imam Sharani says: «If I were to backbite someone, first of all, I would backbite my father and mother. Because, a person who backbites gives his good deeds to the person he backbites, and bears their sins on himself if he has no more good deeds to give.»"

The backbiter, who contemplated these words deeply, came to his senses and promised not to backbite anyone ever again.

The heaviness and ugliness of backbiting is explained in the following verse:

*"You who have Faith! Avoid most suspicion. Indeed some suspicion is a crime. And do not spy and do not backbite one another. Would any of you like to eat his brother's dead flesh? No, you would hate it. And have taqwa of Allah. Allah is Ever-Returning, Most Merciful."* (Al-Hujurat, 12)

Just as a dead person is unable to defend himself from the ugly words that will damage his honor and dignity, the person who is exposed to backbiting is also in a position where he is unable to answer the accusations that occur in his absence. For this reason, backbiting is described in the verse as something extremely disgusting like eating the dead flesh of a person.]

Jafar As-Sadiq says:

"The Muslim who invites people to Islam but does not practice what he preaches is like the one who tries to shoot an arrow without a bow."[79]

[The advice, warnings and suggestions made by people whose actions contradict their words will not have much affect, just like how an empty glass cannot give refreshment. The power of the word is in proportion to how much the person uttering it actually acts on it himself.

For that reason Jalaladdin Rumi said:

"A wise word without action is like a borrowed fancy dress..."

Again, Rumi is saying:

"The one who gives advice by manners is better than the one who gives advice with words." And he expressed that the state and behavior is often more effective than words.

79. Ebû Nuaym, Hilye, III, 194-195; Mizzî, Tehzîbü'l-Kemâl, V, 89.

The Companions were honored with guidance directly exemplified to perfection by the Messenger of Allah, who so vividly embodied the morality of the Qur'an, and by observing first hand, the kindness, grace and refinement of his behavior. It is well known by everyone that people always admire personality and character. Therefore, it is essential for those who call others to the truth, to meticulously obey the divine orders and prohibitions themselves first. Otherwise, they are destined for all kinds of slipups and troubles. Indeed, Allah Almighty is citing the scholars of the Children of Israel as an example in the following verses:

**"Do you order people to devoutness and forget yourselves when you recite the Book? Will you not use your intellect?"** (Al-Baqara, 44)

**"The metaphor of those who were charged with the Torah but then have not upheld it, is that of a donkey loaded with weighty tomes."** (Al-Jumua, 5)

Our Noble Prophet (pbuh) said:

*"I saw some men on the night of my ascension, whose lips were being sheared by scissors of fire. I said:*

*'O Gabriel, who are these people?'*

*Gabriel said:*

*'Preachers from your Community who commanded people to be righteous and were not righteous them-*

*selves, yet they recited the Book. Will they not use their intellect?"* (Ahmad, III, 120, 180, 231, 239; Bayhaqi, Shu'ab, II, 283)[80]

One of the Companions whose heart trembled under the influence of these words and similar truths, Anas Ibn Malik (mabph) explains:

We asked, "O Messenger of Allah! Shall we not enjoin good unless we do it, and forbid evil unless we stay away from it?"

The Messenger of Allah (pbuh) stated the following, "Enjoin good even if you cannot do it perfectly, and forbid evil even if you cannot avoid it completely!" (Haythami, VII, 277)

We are supposed to start to enjoin the good and forbid the evil with our families and ourselves first. In this context our first duty is to raise our children with this understanding. Otherwise, our beloved children will complain about us on the Day of Judgment.

Allah Almighty is also saying in the following verse:

**"You who have Faith! Safeguard yourselves and your families from a Fire whose fuel is people and stones!.."** (At-Tahrim, 6) and He is indicating that we

80. See, Buhârî, Bed'ü'l-Halk 10, Fiten 17; Müslim, Zühd, 51.

should start our enjoining good and forbidding evil with our closest ones.

Raising our children to be friends of Allah is not a simple task that can be achieved by just sending them to the local Mosque during the summer holidays. To regard religious education as simple as this is a very worrying reflection of our own lack of true understanding, so how can we expect our children to get it if we don't have it?. To think that we have fulfilled our duty by being content with this is nothing but wishful thinking.

Fabulous sums are spent and years of dedication unquestioningly devoted to our children becoming doctors or lawyers or engineers. Parents wait outside the school gates with an even greater anxiety than their children during their high school and university entrance exams. What percentage of this huge drama and concern is shown for the learning of our children's religion, which is after all the knowledge they need to pass the exam of their lives; the exam that determines their place in the eternal realm. Let us not forget that the most important test of all of us is to be able to prepare our children well for the divine tests in this temporal world.

Our biggest responsibility today is to our offspring... Because today, the negative propaganda on the television, the wrong websites, the provocations of new fashions and the deceptive suggestions of advertisements, all encourage the lowest aspect of human nature. The ego is raised through the roof with the liberalist principle of "do what you like, indulge your desires", and this shapes the personalities of our children. It is darkening their innocent and luminous hearts and alienating them from their religion, culture, history and even their families…

We all have to take the necessary precautions to protect ourselves, our children, families and society from this sad state of affairs.]

May Allah Almighty grant us the ability to understand our supreme religion correctly and to live it well, to display the kindness, grace and smile of Islam in all our states and attitudes.

Amin!...

# Jafar as-Sadiq

(May Allah have mercy on him)

5

A perfect believer is the enemy of the sin not the sinner. Therefore, he doesn't let his hate of the sin spread over to the sinner. On the contrary, he sees the sinner in need of mercy like a wounded bird who is incapable of protecting himself from that sin. He tries to warn and guide him in an elegant manner without offending him instead of ostracizing him with hatred or insults. He reaches out his hand to his brother in order to save him from the gutter of sin that he has fallen into.

# Jafar As-Sadiq رحمه الله -5-

Jafar As-Sadiq says:

"I never regret forgiving someone! Even if I suffer a lot of damage due to this forgiveness, it is much better for me to forgive than to regret a thousand times for a punishment I have inflicted."[81]

[A believer is a person who gets along well with others. He is a person who tries to get on well with his brothers and sisters at all costs and others get along well with him too. When a conflict occurs, he is the person who shows forgiveness by covering up his brother's mistakes and faults without entering into arguments such as "I am right, you are wrong". It is unthinkable for a true believer to act otherwise because he knows that it is not permissible for him to cut off from his brother for more than three days, and that if resentment lasts for as long as a year, it is as serious a crime similar to the shedding of his brother's blood.

81. İbn-i Abdilberr, Edebü'l-Mücâlese, p. 116.

It is a requirement of Faith and Taqwa to make it up by sacrificing one's self for the sake of Allah whenever necessary. As the following verses are indicating:

**"A good action and a bad action are not the same. Repel the bad with something better and, if there is enmity between you and someone else, he will be like a bosom friend."** (Fussilat, 34)

**"...So have taqwa of Allah and put things right between you. Obey Allah and His Messenger if you are Muninun."** (Al-Anfal, 1)

**"The Muminun are brothers, so make peace between your brothers and have taqwa of Allah so that hopefully you will gain mercy."** (Al-Hujurat, 10)

The following recommendations in the "Emirnâme" (ordinance) sent by the Khalif of the believers, Ali Ibn Abi Talib (mabph), to the governor of Egypt, Malik al-Ashtar, show a high level of wisdom:

"Develop in your heart the feeling of love for your people and let it be the source of kindness and blessing to them!..

They are subject to infirmities and liable to commit mistakes. Some indeed do commit mistakes. But forgive them as you would like God to forgive you. Do not feel sorry for any act of forgiveness, nor rejoice over any punishment that you may mete out to anyone!.."

However, as in every other issue, the measure of forgiveness and tolerance should not be overlooked. Forgiveness, which is a high virtue, is shown to the one who realizes his mistake and regrets it. On the other hand, forgiving someone who insists in disobedience and oppression is not a virtue; on the contrary, it can even be a weakness. Because forgiving the one who persists in his faults and mistakes means giving him the opportunity to repeat the same crimes over and over again.

As Rumi is says:

"Justice is watering fruit trees; while injustice is watering thorns..."

In addition to that, forgiveness is in question for crimes committed against the person who will forgive. However, there are such crimes that attack fundamental religious values, sacred law (shariah) and public order. In such cases, it is necessary to punish, to ensure justice, and to clearly reveal the right from wrong. Because when such a criminal is forgiven, it is certain that this will lead to greater injustices and therefore the whole society will suffer the consequences.

Indeed, our mother Aisha (mabph) stated that the behavior of the Prophet in this regard was as follows:

*"...Allah's Messenger (pbuh) never took revenge from anyone because of his personal grievance, unless*

*something had been violated that Allah had made inviolable."* (Muslim, Al-Fadhail, 79; Abu Dawud, Al-Adab, 4)]

Jafar As-Sadiq says:

"When you see a quality which you disapprove of in one of your brothers, then make seventy excuses for him. If you cannot make one, then say, "Maybe he has an excuse that I don't know of or I can't understand", then close the issue."[82]

[Islamic morality requires first looking at one's own faults and dealing with them instead of looking at the faults of others.

A believer should always wish for good for his brother. He should meticulously avoid ugly habits such as waiting for his brother to make a mistake in order to justify himself by getting into a personal conflict or envy.

As the Messenger of Allah (pbuh) said:

*"Do not rejoice over the mishaps of your brother so that Allah has mercy on him and subjects you to trials."* (Tirmidhi, Qiyamah, 54)

On the other hand, when a believer sees the mistake of a fellow believer, he should not make negative assumptions and reach a wrong judgment hastily. Instead, he should first check whether there is a valid ex-

82. Hânî, el-Hadâik, p. 132.

cuse for his behavior. For, showing this consideration and having a good opinion of others is one of the manners of brotherhood in Islam.

Allah clearly states **"...Do not spy!.."** (Al-Hujurat, 12), this prohibits believers from investigating the hidden and private faults, mistakes and shortcomings of their fellow believers.

In fact, in Islam, it is an important duty of brotherhood for a believer when he discovers a fault and mistake of his brother, to warn him privately in an appropriate way.

The following incident explains this truth beautifully:

One night, the great Companion Umar Ibn al-Khattab (mabph) was walking around the streets of Medina and inspecting the city. He heard the voice of a man singing in his house. When he jumped over the wall and reached him, he saw that the man was drinking with one of his slave girls. He said to him:

"O enemy of Allah! Did you think that Allah would cover your sin while you were disobeying Him?"

The man said:

"O Commander of Believers, don't rush to get angry with me! I disobeyed Allah once while you disobeyed Him three times:

First of all; Allah Almighty says **"...Do not spy!..."** (Al-Hujurat, 12), and you did spy!

Secondly; Allah Almighty says **"...It is not righteousness that you should enter houses from the back!.."** (Al-Baqarah, 189), you jumped over the wall and busted me, by entering my house from the back without permission!

Thirdly; Allah says "O you who believe! do not enter houses other than your own unless you have obtained willing permission and you should greet the inhabitants…", while you entered without greeting!"

Umar (mabph) asked him:

"Will you fix your situation if I forgive you?"

The man said:

"Yes, by Allah, O Commander of the Believers! I will never return to such bad deeds again if you forgive me!"

So Umar (mabph) forgave him and left the house.[83]

The Messenger of Allah (pbuh) is reported to have said:

83. Harâitî, Mekârimü'l-Ahlâk, Kâhire: Dâru'l-Âfâk, 1419, p. 152.

*"Whoever conceals the fault of his Muslim brother, Allah (SWT) will conceal his faults on the Day of Resurrection. Whoever exposes the fault of his Muslim brother, Allah will expose his faults, until He shames him, due to it, in his own house."* (Ibn Majah, Hudud, 5)

*"Whoever shames his brother for a sin that he has repented from shall not die until he commits it."* (Tirmidhi, Al-Qiyamah, 53/2505)

Our Prophet, who was sent to ennoble good character, never revealed the hidden mistakes of anyone, and he strongly forbade doing so. In fact, he never even looked at anyone's face with curiosity as if he was searching for their faults.

The duty of a believer is to protect his eyes and heart from investigating his brothers and sisters, and to be busy with purifying his own inner world from spiritual diseases.

It should not be forgotten that one of the attributes of Allah Almighty is "Sattar al-U'yub", that is, the One who hides and covers the mistakes. Therefore, a true believer should reflect this divine attribute as much as possible.

It is stated in the Qur'anic verses as follows:

**"People who love to see filth being spread about concerning those who have Faith will have a painful**

**punishment both in the dunya** (this world) **and the akhira** (the next world)**."** (An-Nur, 19)

**"Allah does not like evil words to be voiced out loud, except in the case of someone who has been wronged."** (An-Nisa, 148)

Revealing a personal shame and fault of a fellow believer may cause him to embrace his mistake even more and defend it, thus completely moving away from the door of repentance. Therefore, the most correct course of action is to approach our brothers and sisters in a non-judgmental and constructive manner instead of excluding them and leaving them alone with their mistakes and faults. It is to warn with wise words, good advice and appropriate language. This is also a manifestation of the Creator's way of dealing with His creation with mercy and compassion.

For a perfect believer is the enemy of the sin not the sinner. Therefore, he doesn't let his hate of the sin spread over to the sinner. On the contrary, he sees the sinner in need of mercy like a wounded bird who is incapable of protecting himself from that sin. He tries to warn and guide him in an elegant manner without offending him instead of ostracizing him with hatred or insults. He reaches out his hand to his brother in order to save him from the gutter of sin that he has fallen into. He tries to win him over with forgiveness and tolerance.

What a beautiful example is the following incident reported by Yazid Ibn Asam regarding how we should approach our fellow believers who are weighed down by their wrong actions:

There was a powerful and influential person from the people of Damascus. He used to visit Umar (mabph) from time to time. Umar (mabph) did not see that person for a while so he asked the people around him, saying:

"What happened to that person, I haven't seen him for a while?"

They answered:

"O Commander of the Believers! He lost himself to alcohol."

Umar Ibn al-Khattab called his clerk and said:

"Write this down! From Umar to the concerned person! Peace be upon you! He is the Forgiver of sin, the Acceptor of repentance, the Severe in punishment, the Bestower (of favors), none has the right to be worshipped but Him and to Him is the final return."

Umar (mabph) turned to his friends after dictating the letter and said to them:

"Pray for your brother so that he turns to Allah and Allah accepts his repentance!"

That person read the verse **"He is The Forgiver of sin, the Acceptor of repentance, the Severe in punishment…"** (Al-Mumin, 3) mentioned in the letter of Umar Ibn al-Khattab again and again, and he said:

"Allah frightened me with His punishment and He has promised to forgive my sins." He cried and repented seriously.

When Umar (mabph) heard about the repentance of that person, he said:

*"When you see that one of your brothers has gone astray and got caught up in wrong doing, try to bring him back to the right path and make him hopeful of Allah's forgiveness. Pray to Allah for his repentance. Do not assist Shaytan against him by cursing him."* (Ibn Kathir, Tafsir, IV, 76)]

Jafar As-Sadiq said:

"The wrong action which starts with fear and ends with forgiveness brings the servant closer to God. The good action that starts with confidence and ends with arrogance, takes the servant away from God Almighty. The smug obedient person is actually disobedient. The disobedient one who asks forgiveness is indeed obedient to the truth."[84]

84. Attâr, Tezkire, p. 55.

[When Shaytan disobeyed the order of Allah Almighty and committed the first disobedience against Him, he became the prisoner of his arrogance and envy, he insisted on his mistake, and became the victim of his stubbornness. Thus, he was cursed by Allah Almighty.

On the other hand, Adam (pbuh) and Hawa, disobeyed the divine order by following Shaytan and tasting from the fruit of the forbidden tree. But they immediately confessed the truth instead of trying to cover up their mistake.

**"They said, 'Our Lord, we have wronged ourselves. If You do not forgive us and have mercy on us, we will be among the lost."** (Al-A'raf, 23)

They turned away from their mistake in embarrassment, and they took refuge in the mercy and forgiveness of Allah. They were granted divine grace when their sincere repentance was accepted. In this way, they were the example to all mankind, who would follow after them from their lineage until the end of time, about how to be when they cannot protect themselves from falling into sins.

It is impossible for the son of Adam, who was sent to this world to be tested by the two great enemies of his own ego and Shaytan, to remain completely safe and clean from mistakes and forgetfulness. The important thing is to not forget that there is a forgiving

Lord, and make a serious and sincere effort for the forgiveness of one's sin and the correction of the mistake; without ever losing hope in the overflowing mercy of Allah.

There are many sinners who shed sincere tears of repentance for what they have done and as a result, become beloved to Allah Almighty. On the other hand, there are many worshipers who consider themselves to be heavenly people but actually incur divine anger on account of becoming arrogant; admiring themselves and their deeds and feeling self-sufficient.

Many sinners, who are despised, may one day repent and reach much higher ranks than those who despised them. On the other hand, many worshipers who live in Zuhd (asceticism) and Taqwa may destroy their hereafter by falling into the traps of the Nafs (ego) and Shaytan, even though they appeared to be on the side of the truth.

No one has the guarantee of exhaling their last breath with Faith except the Prophets and the ones that they confirm.

How exemplary is the following incident reported by the Messenger of Allah (pbuh):

*"Someone said:*

*Allah would not forgive such and such (person).*

*Thereupon Allah the Exalted and Glorious, said:*

*'Who is he who adjures about Me that I would not grant pardon to so and so; I have granted pardon to so and so and blotted out his deeds!"* (Muslim, Birr, 137)

This means that we must be extremely careful when speaking about matters that only Allah Almighty knows, and we must meticulously avoid saying anything that oversteps the limits. Let us not forget that only Allah knows how and who will accomplish the test of servitude in this world. In this respect, a perfect believer;

- can never be spoiled by looking at his beautiful state and good deeds,

- cannot act haughtily as if he is sure of his fate,

- cannot indirectly engage in self-glorifying attitudes by despising people because of their mistakes and faults…

Again, the following incident reported by the Messenger of Allah (pbuh) is an important warning in this regard:

*"There were two men among the Banu Isra'il (children of Israel), who were striving for the same goal. One of them would commit wrong actions and the other would strive to do his best in the world. The man who exerted himself in worship continued to see the other*

*drowning in sins. He would say, 'refrain from sinning'. One day he found him in the same state and told him to refrain again.*

*He said, 'leave me alone with my Lord. Have you been sent as a watchman over me?'*

*The other one replied, 'I swear by God that Allah will not forgive you, nor he will admit you to Paradise!'*

*Then their souls were taken back by Allah, and they met the Lord of all the worlds.*

*Allah said to the man who had striven hard in worship, 'did you have power over that one who is under My hand?'And said to the man who sinned,*

*'go and enter Paradise by My mercy. And ordered for the other one, 'take him to Hell."*

*Abu Hurayrah said: By Him in Whose hand is my soul, he spoke a word by which this world and the next world of his were destroyed."* (Abu Dawud, Al-Adab, 43/4901)

Only Allah knows what will happen and what is hidden in the hearts. Our duty is to cling to repentance and forgiveness by being occupied with our own mistakes. Therefore, in this temporal world, we must pay attention to our every state and action as if we were walking in a minefield. Let us never forget that there may be people who we never imagined to have better virtues and qualities than we think we have in ourselves. For this reason, to belittle the servants of Allah, is an ugly behavior that belittles ourselves.

Therefore, a believer must meticulously avoid hurting or belittling any human being or even animal that is created by Allah.

As a matter of fact, it is narrated that the Prophet Nuh (pbuh) was the addressee of this divine warning, "O Nuh! Are you reproving me? It is not Me who created it!" because he avoided looking at a purulent dog and turned his face away. If it is necessary to approach even animals with such a deep sensitivity due to their Creator, it can clearly be seen how great a mistake it is to belittle and humiliate other people.

In short, a believer should not be proud by looking at his righteous deeds and good conduct; he should never think that he is safe from the anger of Allah. At the same time, he should also never despair of Allah's mercy because of his sins. However, he should immediately abandon his mistakes and live in a state of repentance.

Allah Almighty is saying in the following verse:

**"And worship your Lord until the Certain** (death) **comes!"** (Al-Hijr, 99) and He wants us to worship until our last breath, poised between Khawf and

Raja, that is, fear and hope. For, it is commanded in the Hadith:

*"You will die the way you lived and you will be resurrected according to the way you died."* (Munawi, Faidhul Qadie, 663)

However, we should never ignore the fact that there might be some exceptions to this rule. For, the Qur'an and the Prophet inform us of those who lived a life in the right direction and lost eternal bliss just one inch from Paradise, and on the contrary, those who were saved from the Fire at the last minute, even though they lived a life far from the right direction.

Again, let us not forget that Allah's mercy and wrath can sometimes be hidden in what may appear to be a small thing. In this respect, we must meticulously avoid even the slightest transgression, and we must strive to fulfill even the smallest good deed and consider it as a great gift from our Lord.]

May Allah Almighty bless our hearts and fill them with awareness of His pleasure. May He grant us all states and deeds that He is pleased with. May He bless our end with His grace and favor.

Amin!..

WISDOM FROM THE FRIENDS OF ALLAH

# 6 Jafar as-Sadiq

(May Allah have mercy on him)

The worldly wealth that is most loyal and beneficial to us is what we have already spent and sent ahead to the next world. Loyal children are the ones we have been raised in the way of Allah and who will serve us as a Sadakah Jariyah (ongoing charity) after we pass away. Loyal friends are those whom we love for Allah's sake and become brothers with in difficult times…

# Jafar As-Sadiq ﷺ -5-

Jafar As-Sadiq says:

"Whoever fights (mujahadah) against his ego for the sake of his ego will attain karamaat (supernatural wonders). And whoever fights against his ego for the sake of Allah, will reach Allah"[85]

[Mujahadah is the fight against the Nafs (lower self or ego)in order to purify it from blameworthy and unwanted characteristics. In this way, it is to prepare the ground for the development of spiritual gifts by resisting the excessive desires and passions of the ego.

The aim of Sayr al-Suluk, which can be explained as the journey of spiritual development, is not to reach some extraordinary states, but to reach a "qalbun salim" (sound or pure heart), that is, to reach a purity of heart that Allah will be pleased with. Otherwise, even

85. Ferîdüddîn Attâr, Tezkiretü'l-Evliyâ, p. 56.

the Indian yogis can obtain some spiritual power with certain diets and disciplines.

Some manifestations, revelations, discoveries and inspirations may occur as a result of taking on this struggle and applying some particular spiritual practices in the journey of spiritual training. These are not the main purpose. This is just a stage on the journey that will serve as a step towards realizing the end goal and is not to be mistaken for the goal itself.

Indeed, spiritual development cannot be achieved without turning away from the lower desires and obsessions of the self. It is not possible to step into a climate of grace with the intensity of pride, arrogance and envy. For this reason Abu al-Hassan al-Kharaqani said:

"Just as prayer and fasting are obligatory, it is also necessary to eliminate arrogance, envy and greed from the heart."[86]

In the eyes of wise servants, the purpose of the creation of man is, 'by sayr al-jamal, one will arrive at kasb al-kamal". In other words, by observing the beauty of Allah, one will reach perfection.

Giving too much importance to manifestations such as miracles and visions of the unseen can distract

86. Ferîdüddîn Attâr, Tezkiretü'l-Evliyâ, p. 629.

a person from his original purpose, which is the ultimate union with God.

The one who forgets his main purpose cannot reach his destination. This mistake is like getting obsessed with sustenance and forgetting the Sustainer. It is the foolishness of mistaking those temporary stations along the road as the real homeland.

The fact that the heart becomes preoccupied with manifestations such as these also indicates the lack of spiritual depth of that person.

The friends of Allah are people with high spiritual capacities. Those great souls can never find solace in any manifestation other than the face to face meeting with their Lord. Therefore, even if they experience extraordinary things such as miracles and divine unveilings, they do not fall into complacency on account of them. On the contrary, they continue to serve with an increasing effort until their last breath.

As a matter of fact, there is not much narration about the miracles of Abu Bakr (mabph), who is reported to be the best of people after the Prophets in many narrations[87].His greatest karamat was his unique loyalty, his exceptional submission and obedience to

87. See Ali el-Müttakî, Kenzü'l-Ummâl, XI, 549/32578; İbn-i Mâce, Mukaddime, 11/106; Ahmed, I, 127, II, 26.

the Messenger of Allah, may Allah bless him and grant him abundant peace.

Friends of Allah live their lives with no need of these kind of miracles or unusual things, and say, 'I don't need the karama (honoring or miracle) I need the Karim (the Generous, Allah)..." The real karama is to obey the order **"So remain on the right course as you have been commanded..."** (Al-Hud, 112) and live in the way of the Qur'an and Sunnah.]

Jafar As-Sadiq said:

"The real dhikr (remembrance) is to forget all that is other than Allah. Then Allah will fill the servants' heart."[88]

[Dhikr is to remember Him in every state. Performing dhikr in a complete sense depends on the harmony of the heart and tongue while remembering Allah. The value and importance of dhikr made with a heedless heart will diminish. The heart should be disconnected from everything that takes it away from Allah during the dhikr. The heart must tremble and come to life with contemplation of the meaning of the dhikr.

As a matter of fact, it is indicated in the following verse:

88. Ferîdüddîn Attâr, Tezkiretü'l-Evliyâ, p. 56.

**"The Muminun are those whose hearts tremble when Allah is mentioned..."** (Al-Anfal, 2)

In this way, believers who can surrender themselves completely to the remembrance of Allah Almighty are bestowed with many divine blessings and bounties.

It is indicated in another verse:

**"Remember Me -I will remember you..."** (Al-Baqarah, 152)

And in a Hadith Qudsi:

*"Allah says: 'I am in My slave's opinion of Me, and I am with him when he remembers Me. If he remembers Me in himself, I too, remember him in Myself, and if he remembers Me in a group of people, I remember him in a group that is better."* (Bukhari, Tawhid, 15)

Undoubtedly, our Lord's remembrance of us is incomparably better than our remembrance of Him. In order to achieve this great blessing and closeness to God, we should strive to do dhikr constantly with the tongue and the heart. During the dhikr we should abandon every thought other than Allah, so the awareness of the presence our own selves will vanish due to the power of our awareness of the presence of Allah.

The light of the dhikr is as strong as the spiritual state of the one who makes the dhikr. In other words, we must also improve our state in order to get a more powerful effect from our dhikr. First of all, we must protect ourselves from the forbidden and disliked things, and then we must pull away from the temporal conversations and then from everything that occupies our hearts other than Allah.

Let's not forget that the more we truly remember our Lord in this worldly life, the closer we get to achieve the divine reunion in the next life tomorrow.

Allah Almighty is warning in the following verse:

**"Do not be like those who forgot Allah and He made them forget themselves. Such people are deviators."** (Al-Hashr, 19)]

Jafar As-Sadiq is says:

"There is no good in a person who is not concerned to meet his needs by working and earning. A good person is the one who makes a living without needing anyone; he pays his debt with his earnings and keeps good ties with his relatives."[89]

[One of the most important principles of good character is to be a source support for others and not a burden. In other words, it is to avoid being a burden to anyone, but to bear the burden of others and help them.

89. İbn-i Şemsü'l-Hilâfe, el-Âdâbü'n-Nâfia, p. 4.

The following is stated in a hadith:

*"The best of mankind are those who are of most benefit to mankind."* (Al-Bayhaqi, Shuab, VI, 117; Ibn Hajar, I, 264)

Again, our Prophet (pbuh) once said:

"Charity is a duty upon every Muslim."

The Companions asked:

"If someone has nothing to give, what will he do?"

The Prophet (pbuh) said, 'He should work with his hands and benefit himself and then give in charity.'

The Companions further asked:

"If he cannot find even that?"

The Prophet (pbuh) replied, "He should help those in need who appeal for help."

Then the Companions asked, "If he cannot do that?"

The Prophet (pbuh) replied, "He should advise goodness."

The Companions asked, "If he cannot do that?"

*"Then he should perform good deeds and keep away from evil deeds and this will be regarded as charitable deeds."* (Bukhari, Zakat 30, Adab 33; Muslim, Zakat, 55)

In other words, the Prophet pointed out that the believer should strive in any case by doing good with his wealth, life, and whatever he has, or at least he can try to be a means of goodness for others.

As Allah Almighty says:

**"Those who give in both times of ease and hardship.."** (Al-Imran, 134). For this reason, the Prophet taught his Companions to spend even in times of need, and encouraged those who had nothing but one date to give charity, even if it is nothing more than half a date.

It is stated in another Hadith:

*"The hand that gives is better than the hand that receives."* (Muslim, Zakat, 97)

Thus, he instructed every believer to be competent in giving and to "be a giver, not a receiver" as much as possible. In short, our beautiful religion, Islam, encourages people to work and earn in a legitimate way. "Hajj" (annual pilgrimage to Mecca and Medina) and "Zakah" (obligatory wealth tax), two of the five pillars of Islam, are made obligatory only for those who have enough wealth. Another meaning of this is, getting rich in a legitimate way by protecting your heart from worldly greed, in order to be eligible to pay Zakat and be able to go on hajj!"

The way of the believer is to help others by working and earning. It is necessary to start from the closest ones. As we find in a well-known hadith, a man came to the Messenger of Allah (pbuh) and asked:

"Who among the people is most deserving of a fine treatment from my hand?" The Messenger of Allah (pbuh) said:

*"Your mother, again your mother, and again your mother, then your father, then your nearest relatives according to the order of nearness."* (Muslim, Birr, 2)]

Jafar As-Sadiq mentions:

"Do not be friends with those who do not keep their family ties! For I have seen that they are cursed three times in the Book of Allah."[90]

[One of the principles that our religion attaches great importance to is to maintain ties with family, to protect and watch over them and to visit them often. So much so, that ignoring relatives and cutting off relations with them is mentioned as one of the heaviest crimes in many verses and hadiths.[91]

---

90. Ebû Nuaym, Hilye, III, 183-184; İbn-i Asâkir, Târîhu Dımaşk, v. 41, p. 409.
91. See. er-Ra'd, 25; Muhammed, 22-23; en-Nisâ, 1; Ebû Dâvûd, Zekât, 45/1694; Buhârî, Tefsîru Sûre 47, Edeb 13, Tevhîd 35; Müslim, Birr, 16.

Maintaining family ties is a matter related directly to Iman. As the Messenger of Allah (pbuh) said:

*"He who believes in Allah and the Last Day should do good to his kins!"* (Bukhari, Adab, 85; Muslim, Iman, 74, 75)

In addition, he gave the following warning:

*"A person who responds to the favors of his relatives in the same way is not considered to have protected and watched over them. A person who protects and watches over relatives is the one who continues to do good to them even when they cut off their ties with him."* (Bukhari, Adab, 15; Abu Dawud, Zakat, 45)

*"Deeds are presented to Allah every Friday except for the person who cuts off the ties of kinship."* (Ahmad, II, 484)

*"The person who severs the bond of kinship will not enter Paradise."* (Bukhari, Adab, 11)

Therefore, visiting relatives, inquiring after their health, sharing their joy and sorrow, visiting them even if they do not visit you, calling them even if they do not call you, is an important responsibility of Faith. However, the most important point to be considered in keeping ties with relatives is to take care of their spiritual situation and to help them towards their eternal salvation. Because the greatest favor is the one concerning the eternal happiness and safety of the person.

For this reason, it is necessary to lead them in the direction of the Qur'an and Sunnah, to encourage them to do righteous deeds, and to warn them with an appropriate language when they make a mistake. It is a very important duty to encourage them to study the Qur'an and hold on to their spiritual virtues, especially in today's world where distraction from the truth is the norm. This state is also a sign of our love of Allah and His Messenger.]

One day, a poor man asked to Jafar As-Sadiq:

"Why do you keep working day and night?" And he replied as follows:

"I saw that no one else can do my job like me, so I decided to do my own job by myself and get rid of laziness. My sustenance has been coming to me ever since I was first created. That's why I have neither ambition nor greed.

One day death will reach me, no one will die for me. That's why I have set out to prepare and face death. On the other hand, I did not see any loyalty from people. That's why I have wholeheartedly chosen Allah's loyalty and abandoned everything else other than this. (I realized that all this was like "zill-i zeval", that is, fleeting shadows and vain dreams, and I gave up any hope in them.)[92]

92. Ferîdüddîn Attâr, İlâhînâme, İstanbul 2010, p. 121.

[It is commanded in the following verses:

**"Man will have nothing but what he strives for."** (An-Najm, 39)

**"Allah does not impose on any self more than it can stand. For it is what he has earned; against it, what is has merited."** (Al-Baraqah, 286)

That is to say, from a hereafter perspective, neither the benefit nor the harm that a person can give to himself can be done to him even if the whole world came together… No one can save a person who oppresses himself by disobeying God's orders from torment except Allah. No one can do any good for a person who does not benefit himself by striving with Iman and good deeds.

In this respect, nothing is more sad and foolish than forgetting al-Baqi (the Everlasting) and forgetting obedience to His commands, by relying on mortal creatures and hoping for their loyalty and help. Everyone and everything is in need of its Lord. Clearly, forgetting al-Baqi, seeking help from mortals and expecting loyalty from them is a deception of the ego.

Those who fall into delusions by saying: "I will cling to a pious person's cloth and he will save me" without equipping themselves with good deed sonly deceive themselves. For, just as no one dies for another, no one will take the responsibility of another in the afterlife.

The following verse confirms this reality:

**"No burden-bearer can bear another's burden. If someone weighed down calls out for help to bear his load, none of it will be borne for him, even by his next of kin."** (Fatir, 18)

Therefore, today we are in the realm of holding on tightly to repentance, forgiveness, worship and good deeds in order to attain the divine mercy and the intercession of our Prophet on the Day of Judgment, when everyone will be concerned with their own troubles.

How important is the lesson derived from the following incident:

While the great mujtahid Ahmed Ibn Hanbal was returning from the market of Baghdad, someone who saw him with his bag in his hand wanted to carry it. When he refused to give him the bag, the man insisted and said:

"Sir, it is our duty to serve our elders." Ahmad Ibn Hanbal responded to him with the following:

"It would be arrogance if we consider ourselves as one of the elders whose bags should be carried and this would constitute a proof that we are one of the little ones in terms of character. For this reason, considering us from the elders will lead us to heedlessness even if it earns you good deeds. The best thing is for me to carry my load by myself without counting myself as one of the elders whose bags should be carried. On the last judgment, everyone will carry their own burden and no one will bear the burden of anyone else."

In this respect, each of us must make a serious effort today to make use of our life's capital through righteous deeds. Let's not forget that this temporal blessing of life in the world of divine testing is bestowed only once. There will be no delay, no repetition and no possibility of compensation when our time is up..

Man was not created for play and fun; he was created to worship Allah and reach knowledge of Him by a spiritual ascent. In that case, it is necessary to live a fruitful life of worship and make good use of our time, which is the most precious capital in our hands.

Doesn't man know that each day a leaf falls from the calendar of his life! Nights and days follow each other, the blessings of the dawn and morning pass over the heedless asleep. Those who live a heedless life in this way will find nothing in their hands when they wake up on the morning of the Day of Judgment. Their life capital that was in their hands will also have vanished. And the little deeds that they did with heedlessness will not suffice for their salvation.

Allah Almighty describes a scene from the state of those who waste their life heedlessly:

**"They will shout out in it, 'Our Lord! Take us out! We will act rightly, differently from the way we used to act!' Did We not let you live long enough for anyone who was going to pay heed to pay heed? And did the warner not come to you? Taste it then! There is no helper for the wrongdoers."** (Fatir, 37)

Therefore, we have to strive to do good deeds that will bring us to a "qalbun salim" (pure or sound heart) while we have the opportunity today, before the day comes when property, children and friends will be of no benefit.

It is stated in the Majestic Qur'an:

**"You who have Iman, have taqwa of Allah and let each self look to what it has sent forward for it tomorrow."** (Al-Hashr, 18)

**"Tell My slaves who have faith that they should establish salat and give from what We have provided for them, secretly and openly, before a Day arrives on which there will be no trading and no friendship."** (Ibrahim, 31)

**"You who have faith! Give away some of what We have provided for you before a Day arrives on which there is no trading, no close friendship and no intercession. It is the rejecters of the faith who are the wrongdoers."** (Al-Baqarah, 254)

Let's not forget that the property of this world that will be loyal to us, is nothing but what we have already spent and sent ahead. The children who will be loyal to us are the ones we raised in the way of Allah, who will pray for us and be a sadaqa jariah (ongoing charity). The friends who will be loyal to us are those whom we love for the sake of Allah and become brothers with in difficult times.

The wealth and property that will fall into the hands of heirs which is unknown whether it will be spent for good or bad, will be of little or no benefit to us in the next world.

Shaykh Sadi, inspired by these truths, advises as follows:

"Procure the provisions of the next life yourself while you are alive! Because after you die, your relatives might become greedy and they may not give charity the way you wish. Remember those who suffer in the grave if you don't want to suffer! Spend quickly to the necessary places while the treasure is in your hands today; do not leave it for tomorrow! Because tomorrow the key will be out of your hand. Procure your provisions yourself today. Don't expect your relatives and friends that you will leave behind to show you enough compassion after you die!

The person, who procures his provision for the next world, has attained a great blessing. Only my own nails scratch my back through my thoughts, no one else does it for me.

Whatever wealth you have in the palm of your hand, give where it is necessary to give! If you can't, you'll bite your hand out of regret tomorrow."

In the explanation of this truth, the people of wisdom have said:

"When a servant dies, he encounters two calamities that he has never seen before regarding his wealth:

The first one is that all his wealth will be taken away. The other is that he will be taken to account for every penny even though it has all been taken away."

Shaykh Sadi continues his advice as follows:

*"If a poor person comes to your door, don't send him off empty-handed. God forbid, maybe one day you will be poor and wander from door to door. Inquire after those whose hearts are wounded and look after them. Maybe one day you'll fall into that position. You who do not go to anyone's door to ask for something; in gratitude for this, do not drive out the poor who comes to your door, do not frown at him and welcome him with a smile..."*

In short, one of the best ways to get rid of the troubles of the hereafter is to seek solutions to the problems of our fellow believers who have been oppressed, and never forget that they have been entrusted to us by our Lord. In this regard, the Muhajirun (immigrants) and the Ansar (helpers) of Medina were the best examples for us. We should measure our religious brotherhood according to them.

We should think about how much we open our hearts to widows, orphans, and our Syrian and Iraqi brothers and sisters in Islam who have taken refuge in our homeland and we should worry and be concerned with their problems.

We must regularly take ourselves to account for our level of our compassion and affection. We should make use of the capital of our lives, which contain ample opportunity to attract the love and pleasure of Allah, through righteous deeds. We must be careful not to waste our lives in the pursuit of vain dreams.

May Allah Almighty make our hearts imbued with the love of striving in His way. May He bless our intentions to be always seeking His pleasure. May Allah grant us the gift to live and die in Islam and to be resurrected with His servants whom He loves and is pleased with.

Amin!

# CONTENTS

www.ingramcontent.com/pod-product-compliance
Lightning Source LLC
Chambersburg PA
CBHW062139160726
48282CB00027B/876
*9789366082080*